STORY MARK

FOR CHRISTIAN SCHOOLS

"With unique expertise and experience, Cochran has written a book that confirms the tremendous value of telling the stories and getting the word out about the Christian school. Found within the pages of this book are stimulating stories and practical content that will not only gain the attention of the reader but ultimately benefit the practitioner in reaching the hearts and minds of potential families who are considering a Christian school for their children. It is one of the few books that speaks specifically to how one can advance a given school's enrollment, by capitalizing on the daily reporting and unfolding of stories that reflect well on an education that is alive, and relevant for today's society."

Dr. Sandy M. Outlar
Ambassador to Christian Schools, Lancaster Bible College

"Experienced parents and teachers know that Christian schools are not knowledge factories. We are in the education business, which is not the same thing as manufacturing. It is not even the same thing as training. Educators have taken on the task of formation—as one writer has expressed it, schools are about formation, not primarily information. This is just another way of saying that education must be pursued as though people mattered.

But that's as far as it goes, even when a school is a good school, and this crucial reality is remembered in the administration of the school and the day-to-day instruction in the classroom. When it comes to marketing that (excellent) school, two kinds of failures are common. Either the school is not marketed at all, or the school defaults to the American factory settings, which means the school is marketed in the same way other products are. Be it butter, cars, books, widgets, or schools, we revert to what someone learned in his business major thirty years ago. But it is a new world, and Ralph Cochran has provided us with a valuable service. He proposes a way of marketing your school as though people mattered, and, as it turns out, this is consistent with the conviction that results matter also."

Douglas Wilson
Co-Founder of The Association of Classical Christian Schools, Logos School, and New Saint Andrews College and Minister at Christ Church

---

How do we cut through today's noise to help 'potential customers' learn the right questions and choose our school, year after year? How do we guard the 'back door' with more effective student retention? The days of mailing out postcards, hosting simple events, and posting a few Facebook updates are long gone.

In an age of sound bites, limited time, and hyper-distracted parents, Ralph Cochran's new book, 'Story Marketing for

Christian Schools,' provides the answer to those who market Christian schools.

Ralph's winsome book begins by framing the right questions to ask. He covers his proven inbound marketing approach at both the philosophical and strategic level but also provides practical tools, including worksheets, to better empower 'word-of-mouth marketing."

Davies Owens, Speaker & Host of Basecamp Live Podcast

"Ralph is 'one of us' in seeking to honor Christ in all things. Thanks for taking the time to write this refreshing, practical, and proven method to grow schools the 'right way.' Go! Fight! Win!"

Larry Stephenson, Superintendent | Logos and Logos Online School

---

"Ralph's work comes from many years of learning and serving Christian schools. Early in the life of Schola, Ralph and I partnered to rejuvenate the marketing and admissions team at several schools. That was several years ago, and the process and coaching have improved since then.

School marketing, like all good marketing, is both art and science. The 'art' is the story that is told through a personal experience that is so engaging that it causes the hearer to lean in and say, 'Wow, tell me more!' My own story of

Christian school is one that includes protection, nurture, structure, and caring at a critical time in my children's lives. The academics and all the other was 'in there' (thanks Ragu spaghetti sauce), but it was these other attributes that made me become a believer.

The 'science' is knowing how to capture these stories and use them to start a genuine and deepening conversation about what is best for the child and their growth into full-orbed disciples of Christ. We want lifelong learners, of course, and we want the future adults to become instruments of grace in a world that desperately needs to see love in action and then to meet the Author of that Love.

Marry the powerful narrative with the ways that the next generation wants to be informed and invited, and you have the makings of powerful and relevant marketing. Use this book to stimulate new thinking, lay down your old notions of 'what works,' and discover that selling and blessing are really not that different from each other."

Harold Naylor, President | Advance Christian Schools

"Ralph has done a great job of putting his successful system into a readable and relatable format in this book. As a Schola client, I have led a team that has learned and implemented Ralph's system for the past two years. We have now watched our school start to grow after years of declining enrollment.

I believe that many small Christian schools are looking for the 'easy' button when it comes to enrollment management. I know we were. Everything was always on the table, from billboards to cable TV commercial to direct mailers. Our board believed if we could just come up with the right tool, we would be just fine. But we found there is no 'easy' button. The secret sauce is the combination of implementing strategies into a marketing plan that fits today's consumer.

To be honest, most of what Ralph presented to us wasn't new. Our collective experience at our school was strong enough for us to understand and have already thought about much of what Schola was proposing. The difference is the depth and systematic method of putting the strategies together. Through our data, we knew that word-of-mouth was critical for us. Yet, we weren't doing any of the intentional implementation of word-of-mouth marketing that Schola directed us to do. We knew that social media marketing, starting with our website, was critical. However, we didn't understand the importance of how this information was presented and just how to push it forward.

This is not a book about theory, this is a book about the proven method to build and manage private Christian school enrollment with a ground-up, workable, and sustainable approach.

You can read this book and go out on your own implementing Ralph's method, and I believe that you would be successful. However, combine this knowledge with utilizing the expertise of the Schola team, and it's a guaranteed success.

Steve Wallo, Director of Development, Director of Athletics | C.S. Lewis Academy

---

Story Marketing for Christian Schools is an excellent user-friendly guide to growing enrollment. Based on years of marketing experience with Christian schools, the author, Ralph Cochran, makes the point that we can no longer rely upon the marketing strategies of the past. Instead, he outlines a new approach to school marketing, including word-of-mouth, storytelling, and inbound marketing. The guide assists the user in developing an effective strategy to achieve sustainable, long-term growth. I would recommend this resource to all Christian schools."

Carol Campbell, VP for Education | Southwestern Union Conference of Seventh-day Adventists

---

"Ralph recruited me as part of his team to found Stratford Classical Christian Academy. We all brought great passion to the effort, especially Ralph. By the grace of God, we started the school, nurtured it, and grew it from 17 Students to over 120 Pre-K through 12th grade. I witnessed Ralph develop his marketing methodology and hone it into a

success. The book clearly presents his proven methods. Marketing success allowed us to build enrollment and concentrate on our vision of building a legacy of Christian leaders. I heartily recommend it to all Christian school leaders."

Jim Luchs, Board President | Stratford Classical Christian Academy

---

"I love the storytelling aspect of marketing. This past year, we really promoted our school through WOM and nurtured our 'storytellers.' It empowered our people to be bold and share our school with others."

Kelly Blackman, Administrative Assistant | Rockbridge Academy

STORY MARKETING
FOR CHRISTIAN SCHOOLS

THE EXPERT'S GUIDE
TO GROWING ENROLLMENT
THROUGH WORD-OF-MOUTH MARKETING,
STORYTELLING, AND INBOUND MARKETING

Ralph Cochran

Story Marketing For Christian Schools
The Expert's Guide to Growing Enrollment Through Word of Mouth Marketing, Story Telling, and Inbound Marketing
by Ralph Cochran

SCHOLA INBOUND MARKETING, LLC
55 New Road, Unit I3, Box 7
Ephrata, PA 17522
Office: (302) 709-1750
www.schoolinboundmarketing.com

Cover design by Marlo Mayuga
Cover has been designed using resources from Freepik.com

Printed in the United States of America.
ISBN: 978-1-7005159-2-6

Table of Contents

Acknowledgments

This book is a result of Rev. Martin Dawson asking me to start a Christian school back in 1999. Jim Luchs and Sidney Henriquez then faithfully helped build the school, and we learned through many successes and mistakes over the years. The cumulation of our experiences led to the formation of Schola, which helped hundreds of Christian schools grow.

Thank you to Schola's amazing team who has passionately and faithfully served the Christian School community for the past five years. All the ideas, strategies, and tactics that are working now to grow schools are a direct result of Schola's team. Special thanks to Sue Carback, Marlo Mayuga, Tera Hodges, and David Pennington.

This book would never have been started and completed if not for Kim Schlauch, who has faithfully helped take my ideas and write them in a way that brings clarity.

I am forever thankful for the support of my wife Linda and my six children, Micah, Laura, Elise, Natalie, Jillian, and Joseph. Also, I am thankful for my parents and in-laws, who have been very supportive over the years.

Foreword

The Coming Rise of Christian Education

Christian education is frustrating. It's frustrating for administrators who struggle to keep their school doors open in the face of limited resources and finances. It's frustrating for teachers who wear a number of different hats, all the while maintaining classrooms with minimal support. And it's frustrating for parents and students who lament the scarcity of sports and dearth of elective opportunities that are all too often characteristic of Christian schools, let alone the parental stress involved in homeschooling.

I know well this frustration. As a Christian educator for over 16 years, I've often found myself despondent, overwhelmed with the inadequacies of start-up schools and the student attrition that so often accompanies it. It's easy to feel a certain futility in the midst of our efforts to recover a Christian tradition responsible for civilizational splendors without equal, which has nevertheless laid dormant for so long.

And yet, something is happening. This Christian educational tradition is currently experiencing an unprecedented reawakening throughout the Western world. In ways unimaginable just a few years ago, Christian education is experiencing nothing short of a renaissance, of which we are at the very beginning. My colleague, Ralph Cochran, understands well this moment in history in which we find ourselves, and he is very concerned that Christian school leaders remain largely unaware of what is coming their way in the next several years. This book is not just about marketing your Christian school; it's about *preparing* for the abundance that lies ahead; it is about laying the groundwork for your school to go beyond *surviving* and begin *thriving*.

I want to show you why the future for Christian education is incredibly bright, and that your marketing efforts *will* pay off in ways you may have thought impossible. In order to surmise what to expect in the coming decades, we need to understand three interrelated trends that are combining to forge an astonishingly fruitful future for Christian educational endeavors. First, our world is currently going through an extraordinary religious-nationalist renewal. Secondly, at the heart of that renewal is the revitalization of the natural family. Thirdly, this revitalized natural family is fueling the rise of Christian education. I want to look at each one of these trends in turn, and then draw some general conclusions for what we can expect for the future of Christian education and the thriving of your school.

The Religious Nationalist Renewal

According to the World Values Survey, four out of five people in the world, that's 80 percent of the world's population, ascribe allegiance to one of the major historic world religions. In sub-Saharan Africa, Christianity is actually growing faster than the continent's population growth, suggesting massive conversion rates.

In the Middle East, more Muslims are attending mosque than ever before in the history of Islam. China is currently experiencing what may be the single greatest Christian revival ever recorded in the history of the church. Hungary's government has declared its commitment to the revitalization of Christian civilization, while Poland has formally declared Jesus Christ as Lord and King over their nation. India is currently experiencing a massive Hindu nationalist revival led by the Bhartiya Janata Party, which is the single largest democratic party on the planet. In the Russian Federation, the Orthodox Church has risen to a prominence not seen since the days of the Tsars. And in Latin America, Pentecostalism is sweeping throughout the region while more Catholics are attending mass than ever before. It's no wonder that scholars believe that we are currently experiencing the single greatest religious surge the world has ever seen.

But why? Why is religion surging throughout the world? The answer appears to be intimately bound up with a renewed sense of nationalism.[1] The nationalist movements today are all united against *globalism*, a vast interlocking mechanism of technology and telecommunications that creates a single worldwide economic and political system.[2] Because globalization eclipses the nation-state with wider transnational economic and political processes, many scholars believe that globalization is bringing an end to the whole concept of distinct nations. Such a dire prospect is not lost on populations as it is most explicitly exemplified in mass, unfettered immigration. As Paul Harris has observed, the porous borders, which serve to expedite flows of goods within a globalized economy, entail a significant increase

---

[1] See my *The New Nationalism: How the Populist Right is Defeating Globalism and Awakening a New Political Order* (Newark, DE: Turley Talks Publishing), 2018.

[2] See, for example, Anthony Giddens, *Runaway World: How Globalization is Reshaping our Lives* (New York: Routledge, 2000).

in levels of immigration, both legal and illegal.[3] This immigration flow trends along the direction of economic activity: Turks flow into Germany, Albanians ebb into Greece, North Africans into France, Pakistanis into England, and Mexicans into the U.S.[4]

Increasingly, the world feels like it is flattening, with one nation, in effect, blending into the other. As such, the cultural uniqueness so indispensable to the perpetuation of national identities appears to be withering worldwide, with a globalist, monolithic, consumer-based culture taking over. Globalism has thus provoked a worldwide backlash, where populations are turning more and more toward their own culture, customs, traditions, most especially their religious traditions, as mechanisms of resistance against what they perceive as the anti-cultural processes of globalization and its secular aristocracy.

The Revitalized Family

At the heart of this religious resurgence is nothing less than the revitalization of the natural family.[5] Scholars such as Eric Kaufmann of the University of London recognize that we are, in fact, in the early stages of a demographic revolution, a revolution where conservative religionists are on course, and these are his words, "to take over the world."[6] What scholars are noticing is that there is a dramatic

---

[3] Paul A. Harris, "Immigration, Globalization and National Security: An Emerging Challenge to the Modern Administrative State,"
http://unpan1.un.org/intradoc/groups/public/documents/aspa/unpan006351.pdf.
[4] Victor Davis Hanson, "The Global Immigration Problem,"
http://www.realclearpolitics.com/articles/2007/05/the_global_immigration_problem.html.
[5] The "natural family" is a term used by the International Organization for the Family to denote a family comprised of father, mother, and children, which functions as the natural and fundamental group unit of society. See https://www.profam.org/article-16/the-family-and-development/
[6] Eric Kaufmann, *Shall the Religious Inherit the Earth? Demography and Politics in the Twenty-First Century* (London: Profile Books, 2010).

demographic difference between secularists and conservative religionists. For example, in the U.S., conservative evangelical women have a 30 percent fertility advantage over their secular counterparts, and this demographic deficit has dramatic effects over time. In a population evenly divided between conservatives and secularists, a 30 percent fertility differential means that in one generation, that 50/50 split will turn into a 60/40 split; in two generations, that would widen into a 75/25 split, and in the course of 200 years, it would be a 99 to 1 split.

Already, demographers are estimating that there will be over 300 million Mormons in the United States by the end of the century, and by the end of the next century, there will be over 300 million Amish! But it's not just the United States; conservative religionists are flourishing everywhere. In France, 30 percent of women are having over 50 percent of all births. Hungary, Poland, and Russia have implemented pro-family policies that are effectively reversing their respective fertility declines. And the Orthodox Church in Georgia has helped their nation go from one of the lowest fertility rates in Eastern Europe to one of the highest.

By contrast, secularists consistently exemplify a low fertility rate of around 1.5 children per couple, which is significantly below the replacement level of 2.1. As a consequence, starting around the year 2030, Kaufmann and others are estimating that the secular population will begin a steady decline to little more than about 10 to 15 percent of national populations. This is what's being called secularism's "demographic contradiction"; their own devotion to radical individualism has become the agent by which their entire ideology implodes.

The Coming Rise of Christian Education

Because the renewed natural family is a response to secular globalism, they're rather suspicious of secularized public education. And so, it's no coincidence that this spike in Christian fertility over the last few decades has been accompanied by a massive spike in Christian education. Just take the homeschooling phenomenon as an example: In 2003, there were an estimated 2,100,000 children homeschooled nationwide, which grew to 2,500,000 in 2009, representing an average growth rate of 7-15% per year. According to the National Center of Educational Statistics, the percentage of all school-aged children homeschooled in the U.S. increased from 1.7% in 1999 to 3% in 2009, representing a 74% increase over a ten-year period. Today, estimates are anywhere from 3 to 4 percent of American's children are homeschooled, which is 2 to 3 million kids.

In terms of classical education: According to the Association of Classical Christian Schools' membership statistics, there were 10 classical schools in the nation in 1994; today, there are over 230. Since 2002, student enrollment in classical schools has more than doubled from 17,000 nationwide to over 41,000. And these are just ACCS affiliated schools. There are estimates that classical Christian schools now number upwards of over 500 in the nation.

Classical homeschool organizations such as Classical Conversations have also thrived, with a current student enrollment of over 60,000. And again, there are estimates that the number of homeschooled children who receive a classical education may be ten times larger than their conventional peers.

We also see among Catholic schools a mass shift towards rediscovering anew the ancient or traditional way of approaching education. A recent example involves an entire diocese of schools in Michigan who have rejected Common Core by returning to a distinctively Catholic liberal arts education. Moreover, we're seeing the development of networks and organizations, such as the Institute for Catholic Liberal Education, and annual conferences that are providing the professional development necessary for a vibrant faculty and administration.

The charter school movement as well, now representing 10 percent of publicly funded schools, is becoming fertile ground for classical education. The Great Hearts Academies currently operates 25 public charter schools in Arizona and Texas, which together enroll 13,000 students with another 13,000 on waiting lists.[7] The Barney Initiative of Hillsdale College has the second-largest network of public classical schools, serving over 6,000 students spanning seven states. Altogether, the total number of classical charter schools may be upwards of 150 in the nation.

And we already see the effects of this kind of education. As of 2015, classically educated students had the highest SAT scores in each of the three categories of Reading, Math, and Writing among all independent, religious, and public schools. In fact, even the SAT and ACT are being rivaled by the advent of the CLT or the Classical Learning Test, an evaluation far more reflective of a classical and Christian education than what is represented by contemporary standardized testing. This represents, I think, the beginning of a real transformation in education assessment

---

[7] John J. Miller, "Back to Basics," *National Review* Vol. 67 Issue 19 (October 2015): 42-44

that has profound implications for what we consider to be an educated person in an increasingly post-secular world. The CLT resembles other standardized tests, but it breaks the area of verbal reasoning down into four sub-areas: philosophy/religion, natural science, literature, and historical/founding documents. Though only a couple of years old, over 90 colleges have agreed to accept the scores for the CLT instead of the SAT and the ACT, and more than 300 high schools across the country are serving as centers for CLT testing.

The trends towards Christian education are just as encouraging on the international scene. Shortly after his massive landslide win in April of 2018, a victory that gave him his third-straight term as prime minister, Viktor Orban announced his vision to build Hungary into what he called a "Christian democracy." Among the distinctives of a Christian democracy, Orban has focused on a renewed cooperation between church and state in the preservation of their national customs, cultures, and traditions; the protection of the nation's borders so as to protect Hungary's unique values; a diverse application of economic nationalism as an extension of national identity; and a renewed committed to fostering and furthering the natural family for a flourishing future.[8] But amidst these grand social goals, it's the reforms in Hungary's K-12 education system that just may have the most significant impact for the coming Christian majority.

János Lázár, a very influential Hungarian politician and member of Viktor Orban's cabinet, recently remarked that the single most important institutions of education in Hungary

---

[8] For a development of Orban's vision of a Christian democracy, see my *The New Nationalism: How the Populist Right is Defeating Globalism and Awakening a New Political Order* (Newark, DE: Turley Talks Publishing), 2018.

are the Christian parochial schools, and he went on to say that the primary goal of education in Hungary is officially now to raise good Christians and good Hungarians. In fact, he made the argument that "the lesson of the last 1,000 years is that the nation can endure only through religious educational institutions."[9]

Now, as part of that vision, Hungary is transferring many of its public schools over to the Christian church.[10] As a result, the number of Christian parochial schools has been growing quite rapidly, especially since Viktor Orban successfully nationalized the schools that were formerly run by local municipalities. Just to give you an idea of the surge in Christian education in Hungary: In 2010, there were a total of 572 church-operated schools; today, that number has more than doubled to over 1,300! Note that the number of church-operated schools has doubled in just a matter of eight years. In 2010, there were just over 112,000 students attending parochial schools; today, their number has reached nearly 210,000. There are even some communities in Hungary that *only* have Christian schools; in other words, the parochial school is their only school of choice. This trend of only church-run schools, particularly in small towns and villages, has been going on for some time now. Between 2001 and 2011, those attending church-run schools in towns and villages increased 60 percent, and after Viktor Orban and his Fidesz Party's win in 2010, that number increased again from 2011 and 2014 by an additional 47 percent.[11] According to a recent study, there are nearly

[9] http://hungarianspectrum.org/2017/09/01/the-orban-governments-penchant-for-religious-educational-institutions/.
[10] http://www.tfp.org/hungary-hands-over-public-schools-to-religious-institutions-2/
[11] https://budapestbeacon.com/church-schools-taking-over-in-hungarys-poorer-regions/.

100 villages and 30 larger towns without a single secular public school.[12] The secular public school is fast becoming the minority form of education in Hungary.

Christian-based educational developments and reforms are happening throughout the Russian Federation as well. According to the Home School Legal Defense Association, estimates are that upwards of 100,000 children are currently being homeschooled in Russia, which would make the former Soviet Union second only to the UK in terms of overall European homeschooling numbers.[13] What is certainly helping the homeschool movement is Russia's pro-family education policy; Russian law explicitly states that education is first and foremost the responsibility of the parent. Another factor that's fostering the popularity of homeschooling is its recent endorsement by one of the most famous Russian Orthodox priests, Fr. Dmitry Smirnov. Fr. Dmitry is hugely popular in Russia; he has a widely listened to talk show where he's a vocal advocate for homeschooling; he has highlighted and interviewed a number of homeschooling organizers and parents on his talk show to help get the word out about the availability of homeschooling and resources for Russian families. Russian conservative Christian activist and homeschooling parent, Alexey Komov, is currently overseeing the translation of the *Classical Conservations* curriculum into Russia.

In terms of Russian public education, back in 2013, President Putin signed a new law, which mandated the study of religion for all Russian students.[14] This measure goes back to 2006 when localities throughout Russia began

---

[12] http://hungarianspectrum.org/2017/09/01/the-orban-governments-penchant-for-religious-educational-institutions/.
[13] https://hslda.org/content/hs/international/Russia/201704040.asp.
[14] https://www.christianpost.com/news/russia-makes-religious-education-mandatory-in-schools-87634/.

mandating Russian Orthodox teaching in their public schools, including its traditions, liturgy, and historic figures. The *New York Times* actually featured a fairly recent article documenting the new curriculum offered in many of Russia's public schools that teaches the basics of the Orthodox faith as part of what Russians are considering to be a truly educated person in the post-Soviet era.[15]

The Republic of Georgia has also been returning to an Eastern Orthodox-based curriculum for its public schools. We have to remember that the Orthodox Church has been functioning in Georgia similar to the way it's functioned in post-Soviet Russia; it's filled the moral and cultural vacuum left by the collapse of communism. So, the church remains extremely popular in Georgia; in fact, surveys consistently show that the church is the single most trusted social institution in Georgia. As such, the Orthodox Church has been instrumental in bringing Christianity back to their public school system.[16]

Interestingly, this re-Christianization of the public school system was actually threatened back in 2012 by the then pro- Western, pro-EU, pro-secular government, which sought to take the Eastern Orthodox curriculum out of the public schools. But these efforts only served to galvanize the Orthodox Church and Orthodox groups such as the Orthodox Parents' Union to mobilize a mass backlash against these secularizing efforts. And so, when the elections of 2012 came along, a far more traditionalist party known as the Georgian Dream was overwhelmingly elected, and they immediately reinstituted Eastern Orthodox education into the public schools. The Orthodox Church in this instance

[15] https://www.nytimes.com/2007/09/23/world/europe/23russia.html.
[16] http://www.bbc.com/news/world-europe-32595514.

became a bulwark, defending symbols of Georgian Christian nationalism against globalizing tendencies that sought to re-secularize the nation. Similar processes are going on in Armenia and Moldova as well.[17]

The Future of Christian Education

Recently, I was talking with a good friend, who over the last several years has entered the grandfather season of life. He is the father of seven, all grown and married. To date, my friend has 23 grandchildren with another one on the way. His tribe has increased threefold, and all of his grandchildren are or will be attending classical Christian schools. My friend's situation is not exceptional; the current generation of classical Christian students, along with new families and schools coming into the classical fold, promise to increase the student population significantly over the next decades. If 3 to 4 million children are currently participating in Christian education, we can easily be looking at over 10 million in the next 20 to 30 years. The trend is one of extraordinary growth. Let's not despise the era of small beginnings; what lies ahead is grander than anything we could have imagined a decade ago. It's time to get ready for the rise of Christian education!

Are you ready? Are you prepared for the coming rise? Or are you simply trying to figure out how to attract the school enrollment prospects you need this year to survive until the next?

If you are ready, get excited. If you are a school leader who is frustrated and struggling, don't despair. This book

---

[17]https://www.academia.edu/17427871/Spiritual_Security_the_Russkiy_Mir_and_the_Russian_O rthodox_Church_The_Influence_of_the_Russian_Orthodox_Church_on_Russia_s_Foreign_Policy_ r egarding_Ukraine_Moldova_Georgia_and_Armenia

is filled with insights and practical advice for marketing your Christian school, valuable information that can help you lay the groundwork for your school to go beyond surviving and begin thriving and also prepare you for the abundance that lies ahead.

Dr. Steve Turley
Author, Speaker, Teacher, and YouTube Influencer
TurleyTalks.com

We recognize growing your school is not easy and even after you read this book, we are sure you will have many more questions and need support.

We have setup a Resource Center with additional content, tools, and a Facebook community to bring you that support. Please be sure to register for it at www.schoolstorymarketing.com/resources and dive into the deep end.

The Resource Center is free for those who purchased this book so please take advantage of these tools and support as you seek to grow your school.

Introduction

Being known as the best-kept secret in town has its advantages when it comes to your school's reputation, but not when it comes to growing your enrollment. In today's competitive environment, you can no longer afford to remain a secret. You need to take action to effectively market your school.

I am going to make an educated guess that as a school leader, your passion is for the education and formation of children and teenagers, not marketing. You have been given a mission and unique vision for their education and are faithfully dedicated to helping parents disciple the next generation of young Christian fathers, mothers, husbands, wives, pastors, teachers, entrepreneurs, and workers in any calling. And you are committed to building a legacy of faithful Christian disciples, one rooted in your faithfulness to our Lord and Savior and, really, His faithfulness to us, His followers.

Your focus is rightfully directed toward the pedagogy, classroom management, and curriculum that your school will use to fulfill its mission. Your interests probably do not lay in developing marketing strategies for your school. However, if you want to meet your budgeting needs to successfully carry out your school's mission, it's something you must do.

To say school marketing can be challenging is a gross understatement. Believe me, I know. I spent 15 years in Christian school leadership, so I understand the angst, the pain, and the struggles that come along with trying to grow a school. And the challenges as well.

Common Challenges in School Marketing

As founder and President of Schola Inbound Marketing, I've worked with a number of schools facing a wide range of challenges when it comes to school marketing. Here are some of the most common I've encountered:

- We are no longer attracting the number of applicants we once were.
- The marketing methods we've employed in the past are no longer effective.
- We need to know what we can do to effectively attract the prospects required to meet our enrollment goals.
- We are at a loss as to how we should address these problems.
- We updated our branding with a new logo, sharper school colors, and lots of print brochures and banners; however, this seems to have had no impact whatsoever on the number of prospects visiting the school.

Can you relate to these challenges?

Perhaps your struggles run a bit deeper. Perhaps your enrollment has declined or stagnated. And perhaps, despite your best efforts, attendance at your Open House events consistently remains low, and you don't know what to make of it. Perhaps you have little or no budget to execute a marketing plan, let alone the people resources required to manage one. Perhaps you lack vision and leadership. Perhaps you just don't know what you don't know.

Perhaps you're a school headmaster or principal who is under pressure from your school board to find a solution to one (or all) of these challenges. Or perhaps you're that school board member who is putting pressure on your headmaster to figure out a viable solution to ensure the survival of your school.

Is there even a solution at all?

Regardless of your role and what you may be facing, I want to assure you there is hope. And a solution. For the better part of the past decade, I've been able to apply what I've learned about school marketing to help schools throughout the country overcome the challenges they face in growing so that they're no longer the best kept secret in town. And I'd like to help you as well.

The purpose of this book is to offer you both inspiration and practical advice to help you shed that "best-kept secret in town" label and grow your school so that you can focus on what matters most: your mission.

Part I, *What Are We Doing Wrong*, explores the reasons why school leaders are facing the current marketing challenges that are keeping them from achieving their enrollment goals.

Part II, *A New Approach to School marketing*, offers a way to overcome the challenges school leaders face through the introduction of a new way to think about school marketing. This game-changing approach can assist you in laying the groundwork to help you grow your school, move beyond surviving and begin thriving.

Part III, *School Story Marketing*, explores in detail the three key components of this new approach to school marketing.

Part IV, *School Story Marketing in Practice*, introduces ways to implement and execute this new approach to school marketing.

Part V, *School Story Marketing in Action*, includes a real-life client example, illustrating the successful implementation and execution of this new approach to school marketing as well as an Action Plan designed to help you apply what you've learned to your current circumstances.

You might be asking yourself the question, "Does this system and approach really work?" Schola has been working with schools around the U.S. and interacting with schools internationally for well over seven years now, and we've witnessed some dramatic results. To give you a sense of the results we are seeing, I've included a series of case studies throughout this book that offers proof that this system and approach does, in fact, work.

Who This Book is For:

This book is for anyone in a position to lead, support, or influence the growth of your school, such as:

- Heads of School
- Admissions Directors
- School marketing Directors
- School marketing Team Members
- School Faculty and Support Staff
- School Board Members
- School Volunteers

In short, anyone who needs to raise awareness about their school, so it is no longer the best-kept secret in town.

Note: This book is written for the Christian School market and is based on my passion for and extensive experience in working with Christian schools. My mission is to help Christian schools, both new and established, grow enrollment in order for them to fulfill their mission to train children up and prepare them to impact the world for

Christ. While the marketing principles introduced can be applied to all different types of private schools; throughout this book, I talk about my commitment to Christian school education and the examples I share are based on a Christian worldview. If that bothers you, this book may not be for you.

In addition, if you're just searching for the latest and greatest in marketing trends, that one trick or gimmick that will lead to instant and amazing success for your school, then this book might not be for you either.

The biggest problem in Christian school marketing today is that too many school leaders are simply jumping from one trendy marketing tactic to another without giving a second thought to their overall strategy nor those they have been called to serve. What is lacking is a deeply rooted strategy that takes into consideration their audience and is designed to achieve sustainable, long-term growth. Because of that, these schools basically view marketing as a task or event-oriented endeavor. As a result, when one thing doesn't work, they blindly go looking for the next great idea as a solution to the problem.

If you are just seeking the latest and greatest thing in Facebook advertising, lead generation, or stand-out event planning as a solution to your challenges, you might not have a marketing problem. What you might actually have is a leadership problem. And, to be completely honest, you might be the problem.

This book is going to be very hard-hitting at times because at Schola, we are very serious about helping Christian schools grow. We all need to remember, above all else, that God is at the center of all of this. Whether you're starting a new school or inherited the leadership of an existing one, you have been given stewardship of a school that has been brought to your community in God's divine providence, and your responsibility is huge.

At the core of any successful school growth strategy is honesty, integrity, and a commitment to the true founder of the school: God. And the success of your school is rooted in your faithfulness to God and His Word, not in the latest marketing tricks and gimmicks.

Because of our faithfulness to God and His desire for His children to be educated in a Christian manner, your main goal as a school is to come alongside parents and serve to guide them as they raise their children in the fear and admonition of the Lord, a journey rooted in our faith and in the authority of scripture. That's where this starts. And your marketing efforts need to be built on that foundation.

So, if your sole interest is in discovering the latest in marketing tips and tricks, I'd advise you to visit your local bookstore or Amazon for the solution you're seeking.

Who This Book is NOT For:

- School leaders who have a "build it, and they will come" approach to school growth.

  What do I mean? I know school leaders who believe that if you have this amazing school culture, then everyone will flock to your school through word of mouth. Although it is very true that an awesome school culture with happy students, happy parents, and happy teachers has a huge impact in this day and age, you need to be able to differentiate your culture from other school cultures in the mind

STORY MARKETING FOR CHRISTIAN SCHOOLS | xxxv

of the prospective parents in order to attract them. That is what this book is about.

- School leaders and admissions directors who like the way things are and don't want to change.

    What do I mean? The Schola School Story Marketing strategy forces school leaders to transform their thinking on how to talk about their schools with prospects and in the general community. This is transformational and uncomfortable. If you do not want to be challenged and don't want to change how you do things, then this book is not for you.

- Schools that think marketing is simply something you do after Christmas break to announce the next series of school recruitment/enrollment events going on from January through May.

- Schools who do not want to commit staff to doing the hard work of School Story Marketing.

PART I:

What Are We Doing Wrong?

My Story

Does it feel like you've been yelling as loudly as you can about your school, but no one is listening? Does it feel like you've tried all the "right" things when it comes to school marketing, but nothing seems to be going right? Are you beginning to feel like, no matter what you do, you're never going to be able to attract the prospects you need to achieve your school enrollment goals?

I know the feeling. I've been there, too.

In 1999, I was asked to start a Christian school. And, simply put, my story is one of just trying to figure it all out as I went along.

Maybe some of you feel that way, too, and you don't see a clear path forward. That's what happened to me when my pastor asked me if I'd like to start a Christian school, and I answered, "uh, sure?"

Little did I know what I was saying "yes" to!

I remember going home that night after dinner with my pastor and telling my friends, "Hey, Pastor wants me to start a Christian school. It looks like we can really help the church, and I think I want to do it."

And they said, "Great, you should do it!" And that's how it all began.

There I was, at the age of 27, before I got married, before I had kids, a bachelor with no frame of reference, assigned the task of starting a school. Where to begin? First, I needed to form a board. And then I had to figure out how to establish a school.

I started reading publications from the 1980s through mid-'90s on how to go about starting a school. And then I got plugged into an association that had a process for doing so. And right away, I began to realize, "This is tough! This is hard!"

Several years went by before we actually opened the school. During that time of preparation and planning, I started putting on informational events, basically what today we would call an Open House or Prospective Parent Night.

Since we didn't have any students yet, we actually imported kids from another Christian school in another state to come up and help us with our "Fine Dessert Prospective Parents' Nights."

When we did those events, it was a real struggle to get people to come. Keep in mind this was in the 2000–2001 time frame, a time before Facebook, a time before YouTube. And a long time before companies like Amazon and eBay became household names. Needless to say, email marketing was not even a blip on the screen at the time.

So, to advertise, the first thing I did was get out my credit card and conduct a direct mail campaign. The printing and postage alone for the 20,000 direct mail postcards advertising our events for that season ended up costing me around $10,000.

I remember sending those postcards out and really getting excited and thinking, "Yeah, this is going to be awesome! We're going to have tons of people respond because I got the right targeted mailing list," which, by the way, was another thing I had to buy.

So I researched and got the right mailing list, spent good money and, "boom," sent out the mailing . . . and then just sat there . . . staring at the phone. And very little happened.

While we did have a website at that time, it was more of a bulletin board where we posted information and articles than a tool for advertising and lead generation.

So, basically, I had spent upwards of $12,000 on marketing for the first Open House, and it was not a very successful campaign at that. While about 10-15 people did show up for the event, they came more out of simple curiosity than anything else.

At this point, I realized I couldn't continue in this manner because I just didn't have the money to do so. We did have some donors, but their donations didn't amount to much. So, I had to figure out a different way to connect with people, and I started thinking, "Okay, what do I need to do? I need to get in front of these people in a different way, one that's affordable. But how am I going to do that?"

That's when I came up with this idea: "Let's use email! Let's see if we can get a bunch of people's addresses, compile them, and send them an invite to the next Open House. And, in the meantime, send them articles from Christian school thinkers I follow who have something powerful to say."

I collected those emails from local churches and other contacts and was able to pull together a list of about 2,000 email addresses, which I thought was pretty good at the time.

At this point, a new company by the name of Constant Contact had just launched, so I got their system and started pushing out emails, inviting people to events and giving them content. At the time, I didn't even realize what I was doing. I didn't label it or even think about it the way I do now.

Through that process, we ended up getting many more attendees to our Open Houses and Prospective Parents'

Night. We were also able to convert those people into applicants, and we were able to start school that first year, a classical Christian school.

While the school was located in New Jersey, a state not prolifically known for Christian schools, it was even less known for classical Christian schools, which is what we were trying to establish. So, we knew we had a tough road ahead. Despite that, we got a decent number of enrollments and opened the school with 17 students.

Over the next few years, the school grew to about 120 students, and we kept repeating that process over and over and over again. In hindsight, I look back and realize I had discovered the "secret sauce," and I didn't even know it. I don't think I came to realize it until just a few years ago.

So that's the story of how I became involved in Christian education. I'm still passionate about it to this day, especially now as a husband and father of six children who are all enrolled in a Christian school. And it's that passion that led me to found Schola. We are committed to helping schools like yours address your marketing and growth issues and overcome the challenges you face, so you can fulfill your mission and continue to transform lives.

Why Schools Face the Marketing Challenges They Do

In the book's introduction, I shared with you some of the most common marketing challenges schools encounter.

While each school we work with faces its own unique set of challenges, one of the most compelling reasons why most schools are not achieving their enrollment goals is that the marketing strategies they are employing are old and outdated. Simply stated, they are relying too heavily on disruption-based traditional marketing tactics.

Traditional marketing is a longstanding approach to promoting products and services through methods such as print advertisements in newspapers, billboards, and direct mail, and through radio and television ads and cold calling.

Once a highly effective approach, that is no longer the case. Why? Here are three reasons.

Three Reasons Traditional Marketing Strategies Are No Longer Effective

1. **The Power Base Has Shifted.**

   Once upon a time, companies and salespeople were the all-powerful gatekeepers of information, and consumers relied upon them to obtain the data needed to make buying decisions. And because these "gatekeepers" were the main source of information, consumers were forced to listen to whatever they had to say, regardless of how disruptive the tactics were. However, the introduction of the internet burst the information floodgates wide open and put consumers in the power seat.

2. **Traditional Marketing Interrupts.**

   I'm sure you've experienced it a countless number of times. You're watching TV, and the show you're engrossed in is suddenly interrupted by a commercial. Or you're listening to an interview on the radio, and, all of a sudden, the talk show host starts talking about sleeping pillows or some other product offer.

As a result of the power shift, consumers are no longer required to rely upon companies and salespeople to obtain the information they need to make buying decisions and, therefore, no longer need to tolerate the disruption. They now have the power to tune out the disruptions of traditional marketing.

This is especially true of millennials, those parents who represent the future of your school, who are completely turned off by disruptive marketing tactics. Why? Because they perceive them to be deceitful and manipulative. These parents have grown up in a high-tech world and have the knowledge and power to turn advertising off through technology such as spam and pop-up blockers. And since they typically don't listen to voicemails or check their emails, it's becoming harder and harder to connect with them.

3. **Traditional Marketing Fails to Build Trust.**

Traditional marketing is mostly based on what the seller has to say, not what the buyer wants to hear. It is transactional and impersonal. There is no established relationship and, therefore, no trust between the buyer and seller. And trust is essential if you want to be heard.

So, what's the answer?

A new marketing approach that doesn't disrupt or manipulate but instead asks permission and builds trust.

A new marketing approach that helps people by offering them the information they need right where they are, right when they need it.

A new marketing approach that blesses and serves.

Are you ready to learn more about a new, proven, and effective marketing approach that can help lay the groundwork for your school to go beyond surviving and begin thriving? Are you a Christian school leader excited about the coming rise of Christian education, who is ready to grow your school in preparation for the abundance that lies ahead? If your answer is yes to either of these questions, then read on.

CASE STUDY:
PROOF STORY MARKETING WORKS AT A LARGE CHRISTIAN SCHOOL IN TEXAS

A 500% Increase (from 67 to 301) in Student Enrollment Prospects in 12 Months and

124 New Students Added (32% increase) in the First Year Following Implementation

Covenant Christian Academy in Colleyville, Texas, is located in a large metropolitan area with many excellent independent, Christian, and public school options for families to choose from. For several years, the school experienced a downward trend in attracting new students and, at the same time, faced a steady slide in retention rates. Because slated school facility improvement plans were well underway, Covenant Christian Academy needed to reposition the school to increase its student population to meet their school goals and financial needs.

While school leaders had been working diligently to sell the mission of the school to the people around them, unfortunately, the message was not making it to enough of the right people. It was at that point the leaders determined their "old school" marketing methods were simply not effective. And, to make matters worse, they realized they didn't know what marketing methods would, in fact, be effective.

"That's when we found Schola," says School Head-master, Keith Castello. "We started doing homework on who could help us and chose Schola because they had both the marketing knowledge and a deep understanding of Christian schooling. And that was the best alignment for us. Schola came in and analyzed how we were going about our marketing and got us on a path to really change the substance of the way our message is captured and pushed out to prospective families. And it's had a very significant impact."

"Traffic alone in our admissions office has more than quadrupled, from 67 to over 301 prospects. And they've been qualified candidates. Not just a lot of people walking through the door, but people qualified by our admissions standards," states Chief Operating Officer Sheila McDoniel.

By the end of the first year working with Schola, Covenant Christian Academy added 124 students, a 32% increase over the previous year. Castello believes this is a direct result of the right message being sent in the right way to the right people. These efforts also resulted in an increase in the student retention rate to 92% that year. McDoniel attributes this to the fact that the improved processes have led to an increased level of internal customer satisfaction.

One of the greatest challenges school leaders faced was the perception that they would need to hand over the ability to make marketing decisions to someone else.

However, once they engaged with the Schola team, these concerns were quickly put to rest once these leaders realized they would continue to own the process. Schola's main role was to serve as a mentor and coach, one that would guide them every step of the way through that process.

When asked what advice he might offer to other schools about working with Schola, Castello replied:

"There never seems to be a good point at which to do these types of things budgetarily. How am I going to carve out the time? How am I going to carve out the money? But the fact is the enrollment coming in the door provides the money. And the money is what allows you to hire the staff and creates the space to be able to do the further strategic work that you want and need to do at the school. And I would just say: Don't wait. Just jump right in and do it."

PART II:

A New Approach to School marketing

The More Things Change...

I recently came across a fascinating and thought-provoking Radio Shack print advertisement from the year 1991.[1] This full-page newspaper ad features 15 electronic devices of varying shapes and sizes. Here are a few of those items:

- A cassette tape recorder
- A phone answering machine
- A desktop scanner
- A portable CD player
- A speed-dial phone
- A VHS camcorder
- A calculator
- An AM/FM clock radio

As I studied this ad, I came to the astounding realization that virtually all the functions these 15 different pieces of equipment could carry out in 1991 can now be performed through one device: a smartphone. My, how times have changed.

There was another significant event that took place that same year. Do you know what it was? 1991 marks the year the internet became available to the public.

The introduction of the internet and the continuing advancements in technology since then have profoundly impacted the way we live our day-to-day lives. Simply put, we live in a much different world than in 1991. And one that continues to change.

Consider the smartphone, for example. Most smartphone plans on the market these days include a hardware upgrade every 2-3 years. While this can be a costly expense, it is a necessary one. The reason? More often than not, due to continuous software changes and advancements, the hardware will reach a point within this timespan that it can no longer support those changes, quickly rendering the hardware old, outdated, and irrelevant.

Similarly, marketing has undergone a seismic shift as a result of the changes and advancements since 1991. If that's the case, how can anyone expect to achieve success with marketing tactics that are old, outdated, and irrelevant?

When it comes to school enrollment growth, however, there is one important exception to that rule.

The More They Stay The Same…

Did you know that Starbucks has a secret menu? I didn't until a Schola team member shared the secret with me. She learned about it while waiting in line at Starbucks with her kids, who discovered it online through a social media site. After her kids ordered drinks from that unadvertised secret menu, they shared photos of their coffee drinks on their social media accounts. This act created quite a buzz that generated much interest in these drinks among their friends.

This is a prime example of one of the most powerful marketing methods of all time; one that's been around as long as people, products, and business have been in existence.

While the specific tactics have evolved and changed throughout the years, the overall strategy remains effective to this day. What is this method? Word-of-mouth marketing.

The need to adapt to the rapid advancements in technology and the desire to harness the power of the tried and true marketing method of spreading the word through people led me to establish Schola's proven and effective School marketing system and to the discovery of a new and powerful approach to school marketing; one based on three key ingredients.

Three Keys to School Enrollment Growth

Regardless of the methods, strategies, or tactics employed, the cornerstone of any school marketing effort is the school open house or similar admissions events that offer prospective parents a face-to-face experience with your school. That said, most school marketing efforts revolve around getting prospects to attend these events.

While getting people to attend your individual events can be a challenge, the true struggle is finding a way to get people to attend your events on a consistent, year-round basis in order to grow your school. To do this effectively, you need to engage and delight your prospects to the point that they cannot stop talking about your school. To do that, you need to connect with them in a way that differentiates you from your competitors.

In our experience, the number one way schools can do this is through word-of-mouth marketing. The second way is through a school website, a tool that is only effective if it is set up properly as a lead generation machine in support of word-of-mouth efforts.

However, the most effective way to do this is through a marketing approach that not only incorporates these two components but is also designed to build trust. One that leverages your current families and supports them in their efforts as trust builders who can go out and talk about your school in a way that can help create deeper connections and pull others in. That approach? School Story Marketing, the merger of school word-of-mouth marketing and storytelling.

A marketing approach that is most effective when supported by inbound marketing.

These three key ingredients have become part of the secret sauce and play a critical role in Schola's School Growth Marketing System, ingredients I will explore in full detail in Part III:

1. Storytelling
2. Inbound Marketing
3. Word-of-mouth marketing

Are you ready to learn more about the future of school marketing? Then read on.

PART III:

School Story Marketing

Having recently moved to a new town, my wife and I had been wanting to join a swim club and recreation center where our family could take swim lessons, participate in athletics, and make friends in our new community. So this past weekend, I finally ventured out to begin our search.

Upon arriving at my first stop, I was greeted in the lobby by a man in his mid-sixties named Bruce, who offered to give me a tour. As we walked around the facility, Bruce enthusiastically spouted out what seemed to be anything and everything he knew about the establishment, including the building construction date, the details of each subsequent building expansion, and information on each and every piece of equipment we passed, including the specs on the recently acquired exercise bikes. While these facts may have fascinated Bruce, most were of little or no interest to me. Having tuned out most of the conversation up to that point, I began trying to come up with a way to cut the tour short. However, at that precise moment, Bruce said something that totally changed my mind; something that made me lock in and listen to every word he had to say thereafter.

"You know, Ralph, this place has meant the world to me. It actually saved my life. Back about 20 years ago, I joined this place right after it opened. You see, I had just had a heart attack. I was really unhealthy and had to change my ways. The people here cared and were committed to helping me achieve my goal. And the reason why I've been telling you all I've been telling you is because I really care. Everyone here really cares about the people who come through those doors, and they all want to help them achieve their goals, whatever they may be. And I'm really very committed to this place because it saved my life."

And I was engaged from that moment on. And everything he had to say thereafter had a much deeper meaning.

As we left the bikes and headed to the indoor pool, Bruce shared that when he first started exercising here, the pool area was gloomy and dark. However, due to renovations that included the addition of sunlights and a children's area, the atmosphere was now much better than it had been. And Bruce expressed how excited he was that the area was so much brighter and more welcoming than before.

Upon the conclusion of the tour, Bruce said to me, "I don't know if this is going to be a good fit for you . . ." But I knew it would be. So, before he could continue, I cut him off, and I told him I was sold.

Bruce's story was a game-changer for me. The way he shared his story allowed me to feel what he felt. And it was that emotional experience that made all the difference.

Your Story is Your Most Powerful Marketing Tool

Never underestimate the power of storytelling. A story can touch people on a much more personal level than hard facts and data can. Data alone can easily be forgotten, but a compelling story can grab and hold the interest of your prospects. And a good story can inspire them to action.

For the first third of our tour, Bruce was focused on the rec center's features and benefits, or what I like to call "technobabble." Unfortunately, in my experience, this is what most schools tend to focus on as well with prospective parents during school tours and enrollment events. Here are some typical examples of "technobabble" in a school environment:

- We have "this" student-teacher ratio
- We offer "these" programs
- We love Jesus
- We have "this" state-of-the-art technology
- We have "these" SAT scores
- We want to build the Kingdom of God
- Our graduates go to "these" colleges

And, like me on my tour, I'm sure these parents are tuning out and thinking they can't wait for the tour to end.

Here's the reality: people don't buy based on logic. While facts are considerations in the buying process, it's usually emotion that influences a buying decision. Logic only serves to justify that decision. When it comes right down to it, in the end, people tend to be less concerned about hard data and more concerned about questions such as "Is this going to solve my problem?" or "Is this actually going to help me?"

The Origin Story

The moment Bruce shared with me the story of how the rec center impacted him personally was the moment that changed everything for me. What Bruce shared with me was his origin story, the one that highlights the moment in time when, faced with a challenge, he had an "aha" moment that led to the discovery of a solution, which, in turn, led to a positive outcome, a story that forged an emotional connection between Bruce and me.

Here's a breakdown of the structure of Bruce's origin story:

The Challenge:	Bruce's health issues
The Solution:	The rec center and its caring and supportive community
The Outcome:	A healthier and improved lifestyle

My decision to join Bruce's rec center was not based on the building's history. It was not based on the new exercise bikes, nor was it based on the new and improved pool area. My decision was mainly influenced by the emotions Bruce's story elicited and the resulting connection forged when he took the time to share it.

What's Your Story?

One question I ask clients to get them to tell their story is this: Tell me in 90 seconds why I should come to your school? And, most often, here's what I'll get: SAT scores, data about class size, the fact that their kids go on a mission trip or that they have a chapel. All features and benefits. All school admissions technobabble.

All of these things are wonderful; however, there may be as many as five to ten other schools in your community with similar features and benefits. To stand out, you need to share information about YOU and YOUR story. Why YOU chose to come to the school. And, if you have children who attend/attended your school, what was the challenge you faced that led you to consider your school? What was your "aha" moment that led you to decide your school was the right choice? And what was the outcome of that decision?

These are the stories your prospects will relate to. And it is through these stories that an emotional connection will be forged. And those emotions will play a big role in any decisions they make.

Practical Challenge

When was the last time you shared the story of your personal journey with a prospective parent? The story of either how you, as a parent, made the decision to enroll your child at your school or how you came to work at the school you are now leading? Your story and those of your admissions team, teachers, and board members provide the foundation for building and creating the change in your school's messaging required to be able to connect with others in a deeper and more meaningful way.

Once you've completed this book, I challenge you to meet with your leadership team over lunch and give each team member the chance to share their origin story, either what led them to enroll their children at your school or how they came to work at the school. I guarantee you will learn things about your team you never knew before. More importantly, you'll discover a bond that can drive your entire school marketing strategy for years to come. This is just a first step of many, but a big and necessary one if you want to harness the power of School Story Marketing.

It's important to take the time to prepare and rehearse your own origin story. Here are a few questions to help you with that:

- What challenge or opportunity led you to the school?
- Why do you love your school?
- How has being at your school impacted you and your family?
- Why are you so committed to the school?

When you share your origin story with honesty and integrity, it will make you more accessible and believable. And that will build trust with your prospects. And when they trust you, they'll be more willing to allow you to guide them through their journey to the point of making an enrollment decision.

The Right Story at the Right Time

Can you imagine proposing marriage to someone on the first date? I certainly can't. I imagine it would be quite a turnoff for many people and might even scare some away completely.

Asking someone to enroll at your school before they're ready to do so is just like proposing to someone on the first date. It can be quite a turnoff for some and might even scare some promising potential enrollment prospects away. So, in addition to being able to tell the right stories, you need to understand where your prospects are in their journey to effectively connect with them in the right way at the right time. And that's where an understanding of inbound marketing comes in.

Your Most Powerful Marketing Vehicle

I previously shared that one of the ways schools we've worked with has been able to connect with prospects on a consistent year-round basis through a school website. And not just any website but one that's set up properly as a lead generation machine. In other words, a website that is inbound-marketing friendly.

Inbound marketing is one of the foundational elements of Schola's School Growth System, a system that involves marketing The Right Way to the Right Audience at the Right Time.

The Right Way

Earlier, I shared some of the most common challenges school leaders face when it comes to school marketing. I also stated that one of the most compelling reasons why most schools are not achieving their enrollment goals is that the marketing strategies they're employing are no longer effective. Specifically, these schools are relying too heavily on the old and outdated tactics of traditional marketing. When it comes right down to it, these tactics are being ignored because they're disruptive. And, because they are impersonal, they fail to gain the trust of potential prospects.

I personally can't stand disruptive marketing and have grown quite weary of what I like to call disruptive marketing sneak attacks. Like that time I was watching a baseball game and during a key at-bat, the TV image suddenly split, and a truck ad appeared to the right of the baseball coverage. Or the time while listening to talk radio when the commentators segued from discussing the political hot topic of the hour to the mention of a computer hacking incident that turned out to be a lead-in for the latest anti-hacking software deal. While some might find these tactics to be quite clever, I find them to be downright manipulative, not to mention totally irrelevant to me.

To be effective in today's environment, you need to market the right way. And the right way is inbound marketing, which is an approach that focuses on attracting customers through interactions that are relevant and helpful. And not interruptive. What's so special about inbound marketing? It's marketing that asks permission. And builds trust.

Inbound marketing is not just a nice website. It is not just an ebook or a blog post. It's not just an email or Facebook campaign. While all of these are important elements of inbound marketing, they're not what inbound marketing is all about.

Just as a stool needs three legs to stand properly, you need to view inbound marketing as a philosophy, a strategy, and a methodology if you want to be successful with this approach. And similar to that stool that needs three legs to stand, you need all three of these—the right philosophy, the right strategy, and the right methodology to effectively and successfully execute inbound marketing.

All the concepts presented in this section are explored in full detail in Schola's Inbound Marketing 101 online course. For more information about this course, please see the resource section at the back of this book.

The Right Audience

Inbound marketing is a prospect-focused approach. So, in order to market the right way, you need to know exactly who you're marketing to. In a school setting, this involves not only a full understanding of today's parents but also knowledge of the type of parents you are trying to attract.

An important factor to keep in mind as you seek to better understand today's parents is that a major generational shift has recently occurred, one that has ushered a new era of parents into the school marketplace, The Millennials. Parents with a different set of expectations, values, and experiences than those who preceded them, factors that will have a profound impact on your marketing efforts. And it is necessary to understand who they are and what motivates them. These parents:

- Hate to be sold to and don't like to be bombarded with irrelevant marketing ads that disrupt their busy days.
- Want to be drawn to your school and feel like they are a part of something bigger.
- Desire to be involved in the educational life of their children.
- Are extremely dependent upon the internet and technology to obtain the information they need to make buying decisions.
- Rely heavily on feedback from people they talk to and those with whom they interact through their online social networks when it comes to making purchase decisions (and a key consideration when it comes to WOM marketing).

In addition to an overall awareness of today's parents, you also need to identify the types of parents you hope to attract to your school. And the ideal way to do this is through the creation of buyer personas, or semi-fictional representations of your ideal parent prospects compiled from market research and real data. In addition to offering demographic details, buyer personas can provide you with the insights needed to develop the content and marketing activities best suited to meet your target audience's needs, desires, challenges, and pain points.

The Right Time

When it comes to executing an effective inbound marketing strategy, timing is everything.

In addition to understanding who your prospects are and what drives them, to be successful in your marketing efforts, you need to know where your prospects are in terms of their journey to making an enrollment decision. Knowledge of the Buyer's Journey can aid you with this.

What is the Buyer's Journey? It's the process buyers go through to become aware of (Awareness Stage), evaluate (Consideration Stage), and purchase a product or service, or in the case of schools, come to an enrollment decision (Decision Stage).

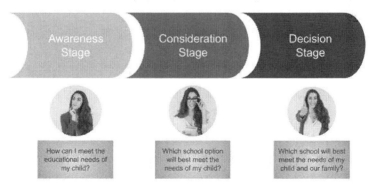

Buyer's Journey

Awareness Stage	Consideration Stage	Decision Stage
How can I meet the educational needs of my child?	Which school option will best meet the needs of my child?	Which school will best meet the needs of my child and our family?

Knowing where your enrollment prospects are in the decision process and what they're dealing with can make all the difference when it comes to offering them exactly what they need right where they are in terms of content and marketing activities.

When we first engage clients through our premium Schola School marketing service, one of the first things we do is try to identify the school's current view of their prospects' buyer's journey. Nine out of ten times, we find that they perceive the buyer's journey doesn't begin until a prospect calls or stops by the school. Subsequently, their entire marketing strategy has generally been focused on those calls and getting those callers to schedule a campus tour or attend an open house.

There's a major problem with this perception and strategy. What, you might ask? Schools employing this type of strategy are trying to rush the relationship along too fast. They're not allowing a courtship process to take place with these prospective parents.

They're so focused on the decision stage, they're failing to recognize that the buyer's journey begins well before this time, and they have no means by which to connect with prospects in the earlier stages of the journey.

Understanding the buyer's journey and how to reach a prospect earlier in that journey makes a major difference and can result in exponential growth when it comes to the number of prospects who connect with your school. We've seen this time and time again with schools that have implemented our system. As a matter of fact, the number of leads a school generates typically doubles or triples within a year of system implementation. And, in some cases, those numbers increase even more.

The Inbound Methodology

To effectively market the Right Way to the Right Audience at the Right Time and achieve your marketing goals, you also need a working knowledge of the inbound methodology, a four-phase process:

- **Attract** the right visitors to your school website
- **Convert** those visitors into school enrollment leads
- **Nurture** those leads through the Buyer's Journey to the enrollment decision
- **Delight** your enrollees to the point that they become your WOM marketers

Inbound Methodology

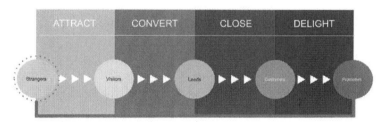

As you can see, with inbound marketing, your efforts don't end with the enrollment of those new families. You need to continue to delight them once they've become a part of your school community. And when you continue to delight your current parents, you'll create supporters and powerful marketers, who will be more than willing to tell others about your school.

Your Most Powerful Marketers

Whether it's learning from the locals where to stop for dinner while navigating through a busy foreign city, asking a neighbor for the name of the guy who mows their lawn, posting a request on social media for a physician referral, or even scanning the product reviews on Amazon to locate information and feedback on an item you're in need of, word-of-mouth marketing influences many of our day-to-day buying decisions. And, more often than not, we may not even personally know the people providing the recommendations we're using to make those buying decisions.

However, it's one thing to trust a stranger when it's a cup of coffee on the line. But how about when it involves a more serious decision?

Consider some of the bigger purchases you've made in recent years. The new car. That rental property for a family vacation. Your mortgage. I'm guessing with these that you might have been a little more selective in the feedback you sought to make those buying decisions.

And then there are the most serious decisions you have or will face in life. Decisions such as which church to attend, where to go to college, what career to pursue, who to marry, how many children to have, where to live, and where to send your children to school.

Anyone who has known me for any amount of time knows I am a firm believer that the choice of where to send their children to school is one of the most important life decisions parents will make. With that in mind, do you think a parent would willingly or easily make the decision to send their child to a school based on the advice of a total stranger?

Consider these statistics:

72% of people get news from friends and family, making word of mouth the most popular channel for sharing[1]

83% of consumers say they either completely or somewhat trust recommendations from family, colleagues, and friends about products and services—making these recommendations the highest ranked source for trustworthiness[2]

84% of consumers reported always, or sometimes, taking action based on personal recommendations[3]

The bottom line: People talk. Friends and family listen and trust what is being said. So, they take action.

And when faced with the decision of where to send their children to school, parents can be influenced by word-of-mouth marketing when the source is trusted.

The Power of Word-Of-Mouth Marketing

"We went to this fantastic new restaurant last weekend—you've got to try it!"

"Have you seen that new movie? It was incredible, and I think you would really like it."

"I just got all my kids' clothes shopping done for next season at this store's clearance sale. You should check it out!"

We put a lot of stock into what our friends and family recommend to us. Often, even if it's not the first time we've heard about a product or service when someone we trust tells us it's great, we decide that we want to try it ourselves.

That's the power of word-of-mouth marketing. When adapted to meet the needs unique to school marketing, it can work just as well for schools as it does for the examples listed previously. And between your current families and other school community members, you have an abundance of potential marketers to help create a buzz and spread the word about your school.

The question is: Are you harnessing the power of word-of-mouth marketing to reach potential new families for your school?

Most heads of school will assert that "Yes, we do word-of-mouth marketing." However, when pressed to define how they do word-of-mouth school marketing, the usual response is, "Well, we just kind of rely on our parents to talk to their friends about us."

Is that an effective strategy? Think again. In most cases, while these schools may be passively benefiting from word-of-mouth conversations, they are not truly engaging in word-of-mouth marketing.

Word-Of-Mouth School Marketing: What It's Not

So, what is word-of-mouth school marketing? The best way to define word-of-mouth (WOM) school marketing is to begin with an understanding of what it is NOT.

For prospective families, WOM school marketing offers endorsements about your school from trusted friends, family, and community members. For school leaders, it offers a low-cost way to market your school. And with budgets already stretched, many school boards and administrators find relief in the fact that WOM school marketing requires a minimal fund allocation.

The idea that WOM school marketing might not require a line item in the school budget can be an appealing one for all involved; however, that doesn't mean this form of marketing will work automatically. WOM school marketing needs to be done correctly to be effective. In other words, it's not something to be simply left up to chance and good intentions.

Do you truly have an effective WOM school marketing strategy in place to impact this, or are you simply leaving things up to chance? Many school administrators have settled into a comfortable place regarding their school's marketing strategy. I'm going to challenge you to start getting intentional about this powerful form of marketing.

Word-Of-Mouth School Marketing: What It Is

Consider the following two definitions:

1. ***Word of Mouth*** – A naturally occurring conversation in which a recommendation of a good or service is given by a satisfied customer to a prospective customer.

2. ***Word-of-mouth marketing*** – Giving people a reason to talk about your stuff and making it easier for that conversation to take place.[1]

Within the second definition, can you sense that there is some intentionality?

Sure, people just naturally talk. However, when you are trying to grow a school, should you simply hope that parents are going to mention your school to their friends at church or on the ball field? Or is there a more proactive and productive way to empower others to join you in spreading the word?

Effective WOM school marketing involves a strategy. One that is well-planned and not left up to chance and good intentions.

Why Do Word-Of-Mouth School Marketing?

Here are three compelling reasons to implement a WOM school marketing strategy:

1. **It's Inexpensive**

   First of all, WOM school marketing is quite possibly the least expensive form of marketing. Aside from the cost of printed materials and the incidental costs associated with helping equip your volunteers, there aren't many expenses involved with WOM School marketing.

2. **It's Effective**

   WOM school marketing is effective because it offers parents of school-age children the opportunity to directly convey testimonials and stories to other parents of school-age children. These testimonials and stories can dramatically illustrate the ways your school is educating and ministering to children and families in your community. They also offer a means for those prospects to see your school as a trusted resource, which, in turn, strengthens the brand of your school.

   As an example, consider the following testimonial from a parent at one of the first schools Schola worked with:

   The summer before our oldest child started sixth grade, I was diagnosed with breast cancer, something most children are not prepared to face, especially in the midst of their own time of uncertainty, hers being the transition to middle school.

Fortunately, while most friends her age in our neighborhood faced the move to a brand-new school building and a brand-new learning environment, our daughter only faced the move to a different wing in the same school building because our school is a kindergarten through 8th grade school. This was a wing she often visited when she was in lower school and one that offered her a much-needed sense of familiarity.

Due to the timing of my chemotherapy treatments, unfortunately, I did not have the energy to accompany my daughter to her middle school orientation that took place prior to the start of the school year. While I was devastated to be missing out on such an important milestone in her life, I found comfort in the fact that we already knew her teachers because we'd been at the school since my daughter's kindergarten year; better yet, her teachers knew her well. I also felt a great sense of peace knowing that she would still be in the same building with her brother, who was preparing to enter 4th grade right around the corner in the lower school wing (a factor, by the way, that tremendously eased our burden when it came to coordinating rides and after-school care for them when necessary).

I cannot begin to express how much the prayers, help, and encouragement we received from the school community during my illness meant to me and my family. I appreciate how flexible, caring, and accommodating the faculty and staff were throughout the entire ordeal, and I am especially thankful for the much-needed sense of stability and normalcy the teachers and students were able to offer my children. Most of all, I am extremely grateful for the tremendous outpouring of love and support the school community showered upon us throughout my cancer journey, a community we truly consider family, and one we are more than blessed to be a part of.

This story not only illustrates some of the benefits the decision to attend a K-8 school has to offer; it conveys the feeling of the strong sense of community that families at this school experience. It's a story of caring and community this parent eagerly shared with friends in her neighborhood, at church, and elsewhere. And one she shared through the school blog, which made it easier for others in the community to connect with and share as well.

WOM school marketing can also be of benefit when it comes to your student retention efforts. The act of having current families hear and share testimonials and stories that convey your school's vision and mission to prospective families can reinforce their decision to place their children at your school. And when retention rates are high, new families are more likely to want to join your community.

3. It Creates Ownership and Community

One of the best side effects of an effective WOM school marketing strategy is the positive attitude that seeps through the culture of your school. This begins with the recruitment of a WOM chairperson and team members that are armed with stories to tell, helpful resources to share, and specific tasks that align with their gifts and personalities.

Your school leadership and other staff members with marketing responsibilities would be wise to enlist the help of a team of enthusiastic parents and other school community members to execute a word-of-mouth school marketing strategy. An effective WOM school marketing team understands the importance of their role and takes their job seriously.

WOM school marketing offers an effective and cost-effective way to retain and grow your school's enrollment. Combined with storytelling and supported by inbound marketing, it completes the recipe for a powerful overall school marketing strategy: School Story Marketing.

School Story Marketing is Not a "One-Size-Fits-All" Approach

If you pay any attention at all to business marketing trends, you've probably noticed that storytelling is becoming increasingly popular in consumer marketing. Consider, for example, Chick Fil A's "Little Things" television ad campaign. Sitting on a red couch, employees and customers share real-life stories of "how seemingly little things have made a big impact" in their lives.[1] The purpose of these ads is not to expound upon the features and benefits of their products but rather to forge an emotional connection between the brand and its consumers through storytelling.

Seeing how the rest of the world markets to you as a consumer, it's easy to think that marketing strategies and tactics that work in the business world can easily be applied to the academic world. As a matter of fact, I've encountered many well-meaning school board members and school volunteers, who've experienced success in business with corporate marketing techniques and mistakenly think the same process would work in a school. Along the same lines, others assume applying the same marketing tactics employed when buying a smartphone or a washing machine or even a candy bar will result in school enrollment growth success. That way of thinking is a big mistake.

To reiterate what I mentioned earlier, choosing a school is one of the most important decisions a parent will ever make. It's a highly emotional decision and, simply put, a big deal. Due to the gravity of the decision, there are many variables that come into play.

Well-meaning though we might be, when we try to use a business world solution to address a school enrollment decision, we do nothing but truncate the decision and belittle it.

I want to be clear that School Story Marketing is NOT a corporate marketing tactic with a "school friendly" name slapped on it, but rather a unique approach developed based on the specific needs and challenges of the school environment. And a School Story Marketing strategy is one that takes into consideration not only the buyer's journey for a prospective parent but the special challenges and considerations they face along the way.

A successful School Story Marketing strategy requires a plan and people to make it work. With that in mind, next, we'll take a look at School Story Marketing in practice through the introduction and exploration of a WOM school marketing plan that applies the concept of storytelling and is supported by inbound marketing.

CASE STUDY:
TURNAROUND OF A SMALL TOWN CHRISTIAN SCHOOL FROM SURVIVING TO THRIVING

A Move From Nearly Closing at 48 Students to 120 Students in 2 years!

Once a thriving classical Christian school, Heritage Oak experienced a sharp decline in enrollment and was considering shutting its doors. Founded in 1994 and located in Tehachapi, a small town in an agricultural and industrial area in the Southern California mountains, enrollment had dwindled to 48 students from a peak of 89.

Some of the contributing factors that led to this decline included an administrator who was not a good fit for the school and its culture as well as a mission drift that led to a derailment in curriculum and a few of its staff members.

Mrs. Amy Walker, who had worked with her husband years prior to founding Heritage Oak, was brought in to revive the school. Says Mrs. Walker upon her return, "Student morale was low, parent morale was low, and even teacher morale was starting to get really low. **When the school board hired me as Head of School, they gave me one year to at least turn the school around and start the trend in the other direction. Otherwise, we were going to have to close the school down.**"

After speaking with various members of the community, school leaders began to realize that many did not know the school even existed, and for those that did, the concept of who they were was completely incorrect. This led to the need to re-introduce themselves to the community and help them understand who the school was and what it offered. Unfortunately, the traditional marketing techniques that had worked in the past were no longer effective, leaving school members wondering how to go about doing this. So, they began looking for resources and discovered Schola.

After the school's first meeting with Schola, Mrs. Walker's biggest takeaway was the need to educate the school leaders and their staff about inbound marketing as well as their target market, millennial parents. Specifically, how are they getting their information, and how are they making their decisions?

Mrs. Walker's biggest challenge was the pushback she received due to misperceptions and a lack of understanding around some of the planned online marketing initiatives. "I remember visiting with some of my staff in the office about some of the plans we were going to initiate with Schola, which were a lot of things through social media. They just could not believe I was spending my money wisely because they could not understand how we could concentrate information through social media directly to people in Tehachapi. Why wasn't it going all over the world? How could it affect just the people we were trying to reach?" According to Mrs. Walker, Schola did a great job in helping them understand the process and realizing social media is where millennials are getting their information.

And once the school began working on that process, they immediately began to see results.

Ultimately, once those involved accepted the fact that what they had been doing was not working and to keep doing the same thing was not going to work, they decided to give it a try, and it really worked. And continues to work consistently. The proof is in the results, as stated by Mrs. Walker:

"We are now into our second year of inbound marketing with Schola, and enrollment is up 36% in one year; the budget has moved from a shortfall to an excess, and there is a buzz of excitement across the campus! The team at Schola has helped us analyze our problem areas, train our staff on inbound marketing techniques, and strategize an implementation plan."

Praise God! After two years of hard work, Heritage Oak grew from 48 to 120 students. They have maxed out their current facilities and have started waiting lists for several grade levels.

And Mrs. Walker is truly thankful for these results. "It's really exciting to see what the Lord has done and what Schola has been able to help us do."

PART IV

School Story Marketing in Practice

To accommodate their growing family, Mary and her husband Randy moved from a townhouse to a single-family home shortly after the birth of their first child. They both grew up going to public schools and had plans for their children to do the same. This was one of the top factors in their housing decision—finding a location with a high-quality public school system.

While in the backyard with her baby daughter one afternoon a few months after their move, Mary struck up a conversation with her new next-door neighbor, who was outside playing with her school-age children. During their conversation, her neighbor, Lisa, shared the story of their search for a private school that could accommodate her son's learning needs. One thing led to another, and Lisa mentioned something to Mary about Lakeside Christian School, a local private school Lisa's friend's children attended and one they were quite happy with. While Mary was not in the market for a private school, the conversation piqued her interest enough for her to file the name of the school away in the back of her mind.

When their daughter turned three, Mary and Randy discovered the local public school system had decided to move from a half-day to a full-day kindergarten program, and this decision would take effect the year their daughter was scheduled to enter kindergarten. Mary, who had left the workforce prior to her daughter's birth to become the primary caregiver for their children, was not at all happy about this decision for a variety of reasons, the first being the subsequent loss of quality one-on-one time a half-day kindergarten program would offer her and her children. Time she had hoped to spend engaged in educational enrichment activities designed to align with her children's scheduling and learning needs. And time she would use to share Bible stories and lessons with them.

Aside from these frustrations, the lack of planning on the school system's part to prepare these young children for such a drastic change concerned her as well. What was being done to prepare the affected preschoolers for the more rigorous full-day curriculum? What was being done to better prepare those young ones expected to make the jump from the traditional 3½ day preschool program straight to the 5 full- day elementary school schedule? Apparently nothing.

The final straw for Mary was the thought of the unexpected yet inevitable challenges such a major upheaval would create and the resulting fallout her child would suffer if she and Randy proceeded with their plans to send their daughter to public school that year. These painful considerations led Mary to begin exploring alternative schooling options.

As Christian parents, Mary and Randy began researching Christ-centered educational alternatives. With Mary's volunteer experience as a Christian education committee member as well as a nursery, Vacation Bible School, and Sunday school teacher, they prayerfully considered home-schooling as an option. However, while they were favorable to the idea of homeschooling, they eventually decided it was not a good fit for their family. Still committed to pursuing a Christ-centered education for their children, it was at this point in their journey that the seeds of that long-ago conversation with Lisa about Lakeside Christian School began to take root.

Shortly after those thoughts sprouted, Mary ran into an old friend at the grocery store from her own elementary school days, a friend whose son just happened to be in kindergarten at Lakeside Christian School. Through their conversation, Mary learned that while the school had an established full-day kindergarten option, Lakeside also continued to offer a half-day program as well. So, based on what she had learned from two very trusted sources, Mary contacted the school to sign up for their next open house. And she invited a few friends from her neighborhood Bible study to join her.

During the open house, Mary listened intently to what was being shared, especially by the school's Q&A panel discussion participants, a group that included two of the school's 8th graders. She liked what she heard and could easily relate to the stories being shared. That night, an emotional connection was forged. However, that's not the end of the story.

Even though she knew deep down that Lakeside would be a good fit for their family, Mary knew this wasn't a decision to be made lightly. She also knew there were still a number of factors that had to be considered before such an important decision could be made. Was Lakeside truly the best fit for their family? Could they afford the tuition, not only for their daughter but also for their younger son when the time came for him to start school? Would they be able to work out the complicated logistics involved in getting their children to and from the school on a daily basis?

Throughout the course of the months to follow, Mary and Randy did what was necessary to answer those questions. They visited other local Christian schools, confirming for

STORY MARKETING FOR CHRISTIAN SCHOOLS | 83

them that Lakeside was indeed the best fit for them. With information the school provided along with some assistance offered by family members, they were able to address their financial concerns. And upon discovering two families in their neighborhood were also planning to enroll their children at Lakeside, Mary and Randy were able to coordinate a carpool to meet their transportation needs. And the outcome? The year her daughter started kindergarten, it was at Lakeside Christian School.

Despite the fact that they initially had no intention of sending their children to a private school, through trusted friends, Mary and Randy gained the information they would eventually need to lead them to Lakeside Christian School's open house, an experience that helped guide them in their decision to further explore and eventually enroll at Lakeside. A school community the family was excited to become a part of and one in which their children flourished.

The Practice of School Story Marketing

It's time now to move from School Story Marketing concept to practice. A practice that employs a story-driven WOM school marketing plan and one supported by inbound marketing. However, before we move on, I want to touch upon three elements of storytelling, elements critical to the success of any School Story Marketing effort:

1. The Hero
2. The Journey
3. The Transformation

Mary's story can lend some perspective on these elements.

1. The Hero

In the opening story, notice that Mary is the hero, not Lakeside Christian.

School Story Marketing is a prospect-focused approach. This means the hero in your story is your prospect, not your school. To create a connection with your prospects, you want to invite them into a story that they can identify with and relate to.

With School Story Marketing, your school serves as the mentor. Your prospects are not looking for another hero; they're looking for a guide to help them through their buyer's journey. Let's take a look at Mary's story within the context of that buyer's journey:

Awareness Stage: This is the point at which prospects realize they have a problem. The question they face at this stage is, "How can I meet the educational needs of my child?"

In our story, Mary and Randy realize they have a problem when they come to the conclusion that the public school's decision to transition to a full-day program conflicted with their values, needs, and desires.

Consideration Stage: At this stage, the prospect defines their problem and researches options to solve it. The main question at this stage is, "Which schooling option will best meet the needs of my child?"

For Mary and Randy, they determine that public school is no longer an option for their family and decide to pursue one that aligns with their desire for a Christ-centered education for their children.

Decision Stage: This is the stage at which a prospect chooses a solution, the main question being, "Which school will best meet the needs of my child and our family?"

Having ruled out homeschooling as an option, Mary and Randy's journey leads them to pursue a private Christian school to meet their educational needs. And after comparing the choice of several different schools against their needs and desires, they decide to enroll their children at Lakeside Christian School.

Understanding where your prospects are in the buyer's journey and what specific challenges they face at each stage can help establish your credibility as a guide. Why? Because it puts you in the position to be able to meet your prospects where they are with stories they can relate to and emotionally connect with.

2. The Journey

Mary's story eventually became her origin story, the one she shared with others in her role as a delighted community member and word-of-mouth marketer for Lakeside. As a review, let's take a look at the breakdown of this origin story:

The Challenge:	The frustrating decision by the public school system that triggered Mary and Randy's need to seek an educational alternative for their children.
The Solution:	An educational alternative that met the needs and desires of Mary and Randy's family.
The Outcome:	Satisfied parents and flourishing children.

An origin story tells not one but actually two journeys.

First, there is the external journey, a journey in which the hero sets out to achieve a goal. Mary's external journey involved her quest to find an educational solution that met her family's needs and desires. A journey that ended when she found her solution in the form of Lakeside Christian School.

The second is the internal journey. A journey in which the hero undergoes a transformation. One in which old beliefs are challenged and eventually replaced with new ones. And this is the journey that matters most. In Mary's case, she originally believed a public school education was an adequate choice for their children. That belief was challenged when a decision was made by the school system that flew in the face of Mary and Randy's values. This decision prompted them to challenge their original beliefs and eventually led them to adopt the new belief that a Christ-centered education at a private Christian school was the best choice for their family.

3. The Transformation

The transformation is the heart and soul of any School Story Marketing storytelling effort; the transformation that results from the death of an old belief system and the adoption of a new one. Your goal as a School Story Marketer is to shatter the false beliefs of your prospects to enable them to adopt the new beliefs needed to fulfill their internal journey. And storytelling is a powerful way to knock down those false beliefs. When Mary had first heard of Lakeside Christian School, she still held firmly to her old beliefs that a public school was the right choice for her children and wasn't ready to begin entertaining the idea of Lakeside Christian until her old beliefs were shattered.

We all create false beliefs to support the decisions we make. We often develop them to protect ourselves and, in many cases, as a way to convince ourselves why something won't work for us. False beliefs are typically born from experience. And in an effort to process the experience's meaning, our minds turn that experience into a story. It is that story that becomes our false belief.

As an example, I have an acquaintance who adamantly refused to dine at a very popular local restaurant because he believed the food was bad and the service was poor. Knowing this to be untrue, I asked him a few questions and discovered his beliefs were based on a visit he paid to the restaurant when it first opened.

Understanding the origin of his false beliefs and having had a similar experience at the same restaurant, I was able to share my experiences with him of the good food and service I received at subsequent visits. The next time I ran into him, I was assured that I had been able to shatter his false beliefs when he told me he had recently dined at the restaurant in question and had a good experience there.

Effective stories shatter false beliefs. To craft an effective story, you need to uncover your prospects' false beliefs and address them. As a frame of reference, here are the three most common false beliefs we typically encounter when working with schools:

1. **We cannot afford the tuition**

   Like it was for Mary and Randy in our opening story, this is a false belief held by many parents considering a private Christian school education for their children. More often than not, if your school is the right option for their family, parents are willing to consider any and all ways to afford the tuition. Shatter their false beliefs by telling stories of families who have found ways to do so. Better yet, share stories that illustrate the importance and value a Christian education at your school has to offer to make them want to do what is necessary to afford tuition.

2. The academic rigor will be too challenging for our child

This is an especially common false belief among classical Christian school prospects. I've lost count of the number of times I've heard about parents who falsely believe this. One mother, in particular, Alice, comes to mind. After hearing stories about the lessons and activities her friends' children were engaged in at the local classical Christian school and the good grades they were getting, she decided her child was not smart enough to go there. It turns out her false beliefs stemmed from her lack of understanding of the classical curriculum. As a result, a much better approach with Alice would have been to tell her stories that explained and reinforced the preparation students at the school receive to be able to engage in the lessons and activities she heard about rather than the success stories that only served to reinforce her false beliefs.

3. Our children will not make friends

This false belief is common with families of potential transfer students. This was the main concern of the parents of Molly, a fourth-grade student who had spent her entire educational career up to that point in public school. As a result of their increasing concerns about public school teachings that ran counter to their Christian worldview, Molly's parents began to look for a Christian school alternative. However, since Molly didn't know any students at the school they were considering and would be leaving some very close friends behind if she transferred, they weren't sure this was the right move for them. After hearing several stories about other families who successfully managed a similar transition, Molly participated in a "shadow day" at the school where she had the opportunity to spend the day with her potential new classmates. While that experience convinced Molly that this was the school for her, it was the stories that convinced her parents.

If you want to tell stories that your prospects will truly relate to and connect with, you need to take the time to research, identify, and understand the false beliefs of those you are trying to attract to your school.

These three storytelling elements, the hero, the journey, and the transformation, can be considered the threads that tie your School Story Marketing efforts together. We will delve into these again in more detail a little later. For now, let's take a look at what else you need to be successful in your efforts. First, you need a framework to support those threads and people to do the work. With that in mind, it's now time to explore how to weave all these pieces into a WOM Story Marketing plan.

How to Develop a WOM School Story Marketing Plan

For most things in life, planning makes all the difference. Before you leave for the grocery store, a good way to save time and money is to plan out your meals for the week and prepare a list of the ingredients to purchase what's needed to make each recipe. Before you go on vacation, it's a good idea to check the weather and consider what activities you plan to engage in to ensure you pack the right clothing for the trip. And before you begin your WOM School Story Marketing efforts, it's important to plan before taking action if you want to be successful. We've identified five steps in the WOM School Marketing planning process. They are:

1. Assess Your Current Environment
2. Develop a WOM School Marketing Strategy
3. Build Your WOM School Marketing Team
4. Provide the Necessary WOM School Marketing Tools
5. Evaluate Your WOM School Marketing Efforts

Let's take a closer look at each step.

Step 1: Assess Your Current Environment

One of the first things you should do before establishing a WOM School Story Marketing strategy and recruit a team to talk about your school is to get a read on your current school environment. What is your current population thinking? More importantly, what are they currently saying about your school?

Previously, the role word of mouth plays in the four-phase inbound methodology was introduced. Let's take another look at this process:

- **Attract** the right visitors to your school website
- **Convert** those visitors into school enrollment leads
- **Nurture** those leads through the Buyer's Journey to the enrollment decision
- **Delight** your enrollees to the point that they become your WOM marketers

For your overall WOM School Story Marketing efforts to be successful, you need to maintain focus in all four phases. And, if you continue to **Delight** your current population, it can make your job attracting new prospects to your school a much easier one.

When you make the effort to continue to delight your current parents, you'll create supporters who are more than willing to tell others about your school. If you don't, you might just end up with detractors instead of promoters.

So, how can you get a read on your current school environment? You can do this informally through the course of daily conversations or more formally through interviews and focus groups; however, one of the most efficient and effective ways to get a read on your current population is by conducting a school climate survey.

The purpose of a climate survey is to provide you with data collected from your current parent population that can help you assess perceptions and identify specific strengths and weaknesses within your school. In addition to providing you with the information you need to develop a WOM School Story Marketing strategy, a survey is a great retention tool as well.

Here are a few questions to consider when creating a survey:

- What were your expectations upon enrolling at our school?
- Are those expectations being met?
- Have your expectations changed since you enrolled? If so, how?
- Are you satisfied with the education your children are receiving?
- Are your children comfortable in their learning environment and do they understand the expectations of them?
- What are your perceptions of the school?
- What are your perceptions of the school community?

One fail-safe tool in determining the climate of your current school community is a Net Promoter Score (NPS) survey question. NPS is a management tool used to gauge customer loyalty. NPS was introduced by one of its developers, business strategist, Fred Reichheld, in a 2003 Harvard Business Review article titled "One Number You Need to Grow."[1]

Simply put, the NPS is a metric that reveals customer loyalty based on responses to a single question:

How likely is it that you would recommend our school to a friend or family member?

Responses are typically provided on a scale of 1 to 10 and then compiled to form your school's NPS index.

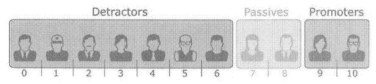

Your NPS can range from -100 (everyone is a detractor) to +100 (everyone is a promoter). Your score indicates the willingness of your current parents to recommend your school to others, which can help you gauge your community's overall satisfaction with and loyalty to your school.

Regardless of how you collect the information you require, your administration may need to do some serious soul-searching as you assess the data to determine whether you are effectively carrying out your school's mission to the community. And, if not, decide what to do about it.

You don't need to solve every problem that may arise before you start to get intentional about WOM School Story Marketing. However, you do need to offer your parents the reassurance that their voices have been heard and steps are being taken to solve problems and address concerns. One way to do this is by building trust.

What are some ways in which you can build trust among your community? Here are a few thoughts:

Identify Problems and Offer a Plan For Solution

You know the old saying, "If you're not part of the solution, you're part of the problem." Make it a habit to be proactive in identifying and addressing issues as they arise.

Follow Through on Your Promises

If you've promised to take steps to address identified problems and concerns, then take action and be sure to communicate your progress.

Be Transparent

Attempts to shove issues under the rug can backfire. And evasiveness only fuels speculation, which is prime fodder for the rumor mill. While it is not necessary to share the details of a situation or issue, it is important to remain open and accountable to your school community.

For example, we've worked with a number of schools that have had to deal with difficult staffing decisions, be it for budget reasons or that

long-tenured employees were simply no longer effective in their roles. While some school administrators received backlash for keeping employees, others received it for letting them go. In most of these cases, it was not the decision itself that caused the friction, but rather the way in which the decision was or, more to the point, was not communicated. This friction could have been avoided with communication and transparency.

Be Positive

Remember, positivity is contagious! Be a role model and strive to maintain an attitude of positivity around others.

Inventory the Things You Are Doing Well and Highlight Them

Capitalize on your wins by apprising your community of them. While you can't eliminate all the negative, you can put things into perspective by accentuating your positive outcomes.

Start a School Blog

While a school blog is mainly a prospect-focused marketing activity designed to attract potential families to your school, there are ways it can be used to generate excitement and build trust with your current families. And a school blog can be an effective WOM School Story Marketing tool as well, an idea we will revisit later.

Post On Social Media

Keep your current families "in the know" by capturing moments from daily school life and posting them on your school social media accounts. Whether it's photos from a field trip, a special school event, or even a peek into the school science lab during a class experiment, parents appreciate knowing what's happening in the daily lives of their children. And it's another great WOM School Story Marketing opportunity!

Communicate. Communicate. Communicate.

I cannot stress this point enough. When it comes to communicating, to build trust among your school community, it's important to do it early and often.

Step 2: Develop a WOM School Marketing Strategy

Your efforts in gathering, assessing, and addressing the state of your current community lay the groundwork for any effective WOM School Story Marketing effort. Now it's time to consider your strategy.

A strategy is a high-level plan of action designed to help you achieve your overall aim; in this case, an intentional way to grow your school enrollment through WOM marketing.

To start with, identify your WOM School Story Marketing goals. What types of families are you hoping to attract? How many? From what segment? For example, is there a need for more students in a specific grade or age range? Keep in mind you don't need to reinvent the wheel here.

Now would be a good time to refer back to your overall school marketing goals for guidance and assistance in crafting your School WOM Story Marketing goals.

Be sure your goals are SMART (specific, measurable, attainable, realistic, time-based). Creating SMART goals is covered in full detail in our Schola University Content Marketing course. Please check out the Resources section in the back of this book for more information about Schola University.

Here's an example of a SMART goal:

Increase attendance at open house events by 3% through WOM School Story Marketing efforts within one year.

You'll also need to determine how you're going to track your WOM efforts in order to measure their effectiveness. Due to the ambiguous nature of WOM marketing, it's unrealistic to expect a completely accurate calculation; however, there are ways to get a decent enough read to be able to fairly assess your WOM marketing efforts. One way to do this is to informally ask those who contact or visit your school how they learned about you or by adding a similar question to online forms or other correspondence.

Next, take a look at the systems and programs already in place that involve people spreading the word about your school into the community. For example, perhaps your Admissions Director visits preschools each spring to inform prospects about your school's kindergarten program. Then evaluate each of these activities to determine whether they are the best way to help you achieve your goals. If not, perhaps it's time to focus your resources elsewhere.

As an example, to meet their budgeting needs, one school we were involved with set a goal to open up a second section in their K4 program the following year. To attract the students they needed to fill that class, and they decided to send volunteers to participate in several local community festivals that drew a large population of parents with young children. Unfortunately, not only did their booth fail to draw any appreciable amount of traffic, those who did visit were at least two or more years away from being in a position to make an enrollment decision. With such a low return on their investment, they determined that continued participation in these events was not worth the effort in the short term and decided to focus their limited resources on other, more effective short-term solutions.

Once you've determined which activities to keep, discontinue, or add, it's time to consider the financial implications of these decisions. While I did say earlier that WOM School Story Marketing is inexpensive, you still need to budget for it in order to do it right. You'll need to take into consideration the cost of handout materials, training resources for your team, events to draw prospects to your school and possibly more, depending on what ideas your volunteers and staff may come up with. Based on those considerations, decide what you can reasonably invest and factor that into your marketing budget.

And speaking of considerations, as you're devising your strategy, it's extremely important to be realistic about what you can expect from your school community. You know your parents, your community, and the resources that may (or may not) be at your disposal in your area. To ensure you can set them up for success, make sure the expectations that you have for your WOM team are realistic ones.

And last, but certainly not least, you'll need to carefully consider how storytelling will factor into this strategy. Considerations include:

- Educating your school leaders and other influencers on the value and importance of storytelling so they can help lead the charge.

- Researching, identifying, and understanding the false beliefs of those you are trying to attract to your school and coming up with stories that shatter those false beliefs.

- Training your leaders on the process of developing and sharing their own origin stories.

- Creating an intentional system of story collecting and sharing.

- Training up storytellers, equipping them with the stories you collect, and empowering them to come up with their own.

I'll touch upon more storytelling tactics in later steps that will provide additional insights for completing your WOM School Story Marketing strategy. In addition, these considerations are included again for you to think about and address in the School Story Marketing Action Plan located in the next section.

Step 3: Build Your WOM School Marketing Team

With your strategy in place and a budget to support that strategy, it's now time to identify the people needed to make it happen. Here are some suggestions for building your team:

Find Your Chairperson

To build an effective WOM School Story Marketing team, you first need to identify the chairperson who will lead the charge. This individual should be someone who is a good communicator, organized, and relational. Your chairperson should not be the head of school, but someone who can be trusted to carry out responsibilities with your head of school's support.

Your chairperson will also serve as coach to your WOM team. Ideally, this individual will be able to identify the strengths of their players and place them in positions where they'll be most effective. They'll also be charged with keeping the team on task, continuously feeding them compelling stories, and tracking the team's progress.

Recruit Your Team

Along with your chairperson, you'll need to recruit a team of "talkers," or those who will "love your school out loud." Parents are obvious picks for the WOM team since they're the ones likely to be most connected to the greater community and invested in your school. Alumni parents, staff members, both current and retired, and other supporters of your school are also good choices for team members. And keep in mind that team members don't need to be super extroverts but do need to have a positive attitude about the school.

Ways to recruit team members include promoting the team at your Back to School Night and other events as well as announcing it in your parent email communications or newsletters. However, the most effective way to recruit members is to personally ask them. Be on the lookout for parents who are well-connected and/or enthusiastic supporters of your school and be sure to extend them a personal invitation to join the team.

Assign Tasks

Once you've assembled your team, plan several meetings throughout the course of the year to pull your WOM team together. Take the opportunity during these meetings to share stories about how students are benefitting from the education they're receiving at your school. Conduct brainstorming sessions to come up with ways you can be proactive in taking your school's message to the greater community. And help each team member identify a way in which they can spread the word about your school in a way that's natural and comfortable for them.

One task all team members can perform is that of parent ambassadors for your community. In this role, members can be assigned one or more of the following tasks:

- Writing thank-you notes to prospective families who visit the school.
- Handing out brochures/posters advertising school events to their friends, churches, and other organizations.
- Serving as greeters during school tours, open houses, and other school events.

Support Your Team's Efforts

To ensure their success, you'll want to provide your team with the right tools, which we'll cover next; however, before we get into those, I want to touch upon another extremely valuable way to support your team, and that is by recognizing their efforts.

Make it a point to acknowledge what they've done and are doing in support of your school and let them know how much you appreciate those efforts. This can be as simple as sending each of them a handwritten note or by hosting an event for them, such as an appreciation breakfast at the end of the school year. Your efforts can help keep them engaged and energized, and word of your actions may even entice others to join your team. Now that's WOM marketing in action!

Step 4: Provide the Necessary WOM Marketing Tools

While there are a variety of effective tools you can provide your WOM team, one of the most significant ways to equip your WOM marketing team is by teaching them to become storytellers. Why? Because the story is at the heart of any School Story Marketing effort. And it's that heart connection that will make all the difference.

One of the highlighted benefits a K-8 client school frequently shares with prospective parents of kindergarteners is their carpool buddy program, one in which their 8th graders provide escort service from car to classroom for its K4 and K5 students. While the program might be a nice benefit, it's neither an uncommon nor a compelling one. However, the story behind the program's inception is.

To allow teachers the time they needed to prepare for the school day, it had been a standard practice to have all students who arrived prior to the official start of school to report to and wait in the gym until they were dismissed to their classrooms at the appointed time. Due to the large size of the gym and the number of students it contained, the gym tended to become quite loud and rowdy, which proved a bit too overwhelming for a new kindergartener who was having a hard time with his transition from a small preschool to begin with. As a result of the stress and struggle he, his family, his teachers and fellow students were dealing with, the decision was made to move the school's youngest students from the gym to a cozier and more welcoming environment.

While the move was a beneficial one for the affected student and others directly involved, it led to a few unexpected challenges, the main one being how to get the kindergarteners to their new location in the mornings. For, unlike the gym that provided easy access by way of a door a few mere feet from the start of the carpool line, the new room did not offer such easy access and proved to be somewhat difficult for an unescorted five-year-old to locate.

The recruitment of 8th grade volunteers responsible for meeting the kindergarteners at their cars in the morning and escorting them to the assigned classroom resolved this dilemma and led to a few unanticipated but welcomed outcomes.

Shortly after the kindergarteners moved to their new location, a few additional 8th graders volunteered to assist the staff member on duty in the mornings by coming in to play with and read to the kindergartners. And those who volunteered to escort the young students to the classroom in the mornings eventually began escorting them back to their cars at the end of the school day as well. And what started as a way to meet a basic need became a wonderful way for the school's youngest students to connect with and develop friendships with the oldest while offering the school's 8th graders a meaningful way to develop their leadership and mentoring skills. All from an effort to simply meet the needs of one child.

Can you see how much more effective it could be if a WOM team member shared the story of the carpool buddy program instead of simply telling them the program exists?

Stories not only entertain and educate; they provide the opportunity to present real-life examples people can relate to. Ones to which they'll respond: "I feel like you're talking directly to me!" or "You understand me!" When your audience can relate to the individuals and experiences in the stories you share, an emotional connection is forged. And those emotions play a big role in the decisions they make.

As I shared earlier, a story can also touch people on a more personal level than hard facts and data can. Data alone can easily be forgotten, but a compelling story can grab and hold the interest of your audience. And a good story can build trust and inspire them to action.

At this point, you may be thinking, "This is all great, but how do I teach my WOM team to become storytellers?" First, start by filling them in on your school's backstory. Next, teach them the storytelling process and explain the three critical elements of school storytelling. Finally, give them something to talk about.

Start With Your School's Backstory

Your backstory is your "who," "what," and "why." Who are you and why do you exist? Your team should be well- versed on your school's mission, vision, and values. What is your message? Your school message is what you are trying to convey to your prospects that will make them want to come to your school.

To help them remember and articulate your backstory, provide them with an "elevator speech," that 30-second description that embodies who you are, why you exist, and what you're all about.

Why is this important? When your WOM team knows and understands your backstory, it makes it easier for them to frame the stories they tell in a way that clearly conveys your intended message. And, as they explore their own personal backstories, it provides the context needed for your WOM team to craft their origin stories in a way that can aid them in forging stronger emotional connections with prospects in an effort to help them overcome their false beliefs.

Teach Them the Storytelling Process

The most efficient and effective way to equip your WOM team to tell stories is to keep it simple. While there are many storytelling models out there, some more complicated than others, the simple fact of the matter is that all stories include three main parts: a beginning, a middle, and an end. From a marketing perspective, this process involves a challenge, a solution, and an outcome.

Let's apply this process to the one I just told:

Challenge: The kindergarten student was overwhelmed by the crowd in the gym.

Solution: The action to move and provide support for the relocated students. **Outcome:** The challenge is resolved, and greater benefits realized as a result.

With practice and support, this process can be used to convey a variety of stories that can influence, educate, and persuade. However, the most important story to begin with is the origin story.

Model the process by sharing your own first. Then, encourage your WOM team members to come up with their own origin story using the storytelling process:

- What challenge brought them to your school?
- How did coming to your school address that challenge?
- What was the outcome of the decision to come to your school?

Because it is theirs, this could be the most compelling story they tell. And the most effective. Why? Because it personalizes the enrollment decision process for those who hear the story. It conveys to them that, yes, I've been in your shoes and know the struggle you're facing. And it offers hope; hope that there is a solution for that prospective family. And one that can lead to a positive outcome.

Explain the Three Critical Elements of School Storytelling

Ensure your WOM team is familiar with the three critical elements of school storytelling and how an understanding of them can positively impact the stories they tell, especially their origin story. As a review, here they are:

The Hero – A prospect should easily be able to step into the shoes of the story's hero. This character has to be someone who they can identify with and relate to.

In our most recent story, the hero is the kindergartner and his family. They faced the rough transition from preschool to life in a K-8 school.

The Journey – The story should take into consideration the hero's two journeys, the external journey of achievement and the internal journey of transformation.

The external of our hero's journey involved overcoming the challenge of the stress brought on by the time spent in the large and loud gym. A journey in which the school came alongside the hero as a mentor to help resolve the challenge.

The internal journey involved the transformation of a scared and stressed kindergartener into one who went on to thrive in a different environment. And one who even went on to make friends with some of the oldest students in the school, ones he was initially afraid of during his time in the gym.

The Transformation – The story should involve a transformation, the shattering of an old belief and the adoption of a new one. It should also portray how that transformation affects the decision process.

Since most public elementary schools only house students up through the fifth grade, the idea of sending a kindergartener to a school that includes middle schoolers as well might seem a bit daunting, especially for families of children like the one in our story. Families like that may even develop the false belief that such a school is not right for them. Can you see how a story like this might help overcome those false beliefs?

Give Them Something to Talk About

Stories can serve a variety of purposes in the practice of School Story Marketing. We've talked about how origin stories can forge emotional connections. I've shared with you how stories can shatter false beliefs. We've also covered how stories can convey information about your school on a much more personal level than facts and data can.

Regardless of the specific purpose they serve, stories always make a difference. So, make the effort to provide your WOM team with material to feed the storytelling process. This can be in the form of stories passed along from others, or raw material they can use to create their own stories. For example, give them special insights into your school's workings. Let your WOM team be the first to hear about special plans for the school, such as the new gymnasium project, the exciting plans you have for the upcoming middle school retreat, your goals to start a summer camp or after school program. Empower them with the latest news through occasional meetings, email updates, and one-on-one conversations.

Another way to give them something to talk is to create experiences likely to generate a buzz that can organically and authentically lead to storytelling. How? By exceeding your school community's expectations. In other words, delight them.

Start by reviewing the feedback you received during the assessment of your current school environment. Examine the ways in which you are meeting your community's expectations. What can you do to turn things up a notch? What are some ways in which you can exceed those expectations?

For example, are your parents pleased with the caring and encouraging nature of your faculty and staff? Step it up a notch by empowering your teachers to coordinate efforts so that each student in the class receives one personalized and encouraging note in the mail from a faculty or staff member some time during the school year.

Is there a special program your school is well-known for and cherished by your current community? Step it up a notch and organize a special social event highlighting this program and encourage current families to invite their friends to the celebration.

Another way to exceed expectations is to maintain a continuous pulse on the school environment and adapt your plans accordingly, as school leaders at one school did midway through the school year.

Due to a series of circumstances that resulted in a tense fall for this school community, the environment was somewhat cold and negative. Faced with the additional challenge of battling the negativity of the "winter doldrums," that naturally occurring phenomenon the frigid and blustery winter months naturally bring about, the school administration decided they need to take action to heat things up a bit.

When the students returned from Christmas break, school leaders unveiled their plans for a "Theme Day" winter program. The idea was simple: one Friday a month during this timeframe, the day's activities revolved around a special theme. On each theme day, students got the chance to shed their uniforms for the day and instead, dress according to the theme.

Teachers prepared theme-related learning activities, and a special schoolwide event was held at the end of the day. For example, in March, the school held a "Pi Day." Throughout the week leading up to that particular Friday, students had the chance to participate in a fundraiser for the school drama program. For each dollar donated, students received one vote to cast for the faculty or staff member they wanted to see get "pied." This contest culminated in a school-wide activity that Friday afternoon where students and parents watched and cheered as the top vote-getters received a whipped cream pie to the face.

Not only did this event generate quite a buzz, but it was an experience shared through stories by parents on their social media accounts. And that's WOM School Story Marketing in action through storytelling.

Aside from storytelling, here are some additional marketing tools you can arm your WOM talkers with:

- Provide school brochures or rack cards for them to distribute that list Open House dates and other pertinent event information. Make sure these have a clear Call-to-Action on them, such as details on how to access one of your school's premium content offerings from your school website.

- Have team t-shirts made and give team members magnets to put on their cars.

- Ask them to like, share, and comment on your school's social media channels.

- Encourage them to write positive online reviews for your school on relevant sites such as greatschools.org.

- Host "invite-a-friend" events specifically designed to connect parents and children. Invite non-school families to attend. These can include play dates, seminars, social events, and more.

- Create relevant online tools like videos, landing pages, blog posts, and ebooks that your team members can easily forward and/or share with their connections.

- Provide them with "Talking Points." Keep them up to date on noteworthy goings-on in the school community and encourage team members to seek them out as well. These may be things you take for granted, such as the previous example of the 8th graders serving the kindergarten students but may be unique and attractive to prospective families.

A closing thought on WOM School Story Marketing tools: Many companies offer referral incentive programs, and you may be wondering if that might be an effective tool to consider. Before you go down that path, I want to caution you on a potential "side effect" of providing these types of incentives for your WOM team.

When it comes right down to it, referral fees can make a WOM parent's recommendation feel tainted. And it's likely that your current families are referring new families to your school regardless of whether or not they receive a referral fee. If you are paying for these referrals, you are using budget dollars you don't need to be spending.

Andy Sernovitz, in his book, *Word of Mouth Marketing*, says: *"Offering customers incentives to spread the word about your stuff is often a mistake, and here's why: You make them feel dirty if they've paid for it... When you link a monetary reward to referring your stuff, you taint the person's motivation for talking about it. It's a kind of bribe. Instead of being a friend for recommending a cool product, the person becomes a spokesperson for the company... It turns the friend- to-friend relationship into a salesperson-to-prospect transaction. Even good friends or family members are less believable when they're working for rewards."* [2]

This can be true whether or not the person being referred knows there is a referral bounty on their head. It can implicitly impact the overall motivation of the referrer, especially for a very emotional recommendation, such as choosing a school.

After all, it's not the same thing as referring someone for, say, a car repair mechanic. Rather than give out $2000 in referral fees, you might be better off using that money to host a special thank-you event for your team members.

Step 5: Evaluate Your Word of Mouth Story Marketing Efforts

If you want to keep your WOM School Story Marketing plan working for your school in the long run, you'll need to keep an ever-present finger on the pulse of your efforts to make sure they're working, and then make necessary adjustments as required to keep it running smoothly.

To begin with, ask prospects who contact your school as well as newly enrolled parents if they were impacted by the strategies you've put into place. In addition, ask the volunteers on your WOM team what responses they're receiving from the people they tell about your school.

To assist you in better managing your ongoing efforts, it might help to focus the team on two or three main messages you want to communicate in a particular school year to the greater community. Are there common misconceptions about your school that you can help clarify? For example, perhaps there's some confusion surrounding a recent decision to discontinue offering a once-popular program at your school. It might be a good idea to share the story surrounding the decision along with the positive outcome you expect as a result of making that decision.

Be intentional about communicating a specific message to your community and then, after a few months, survey your families to discover whether they received and understood the message.

In general, it's important to regularly review your overall WOM efforts and ask yourself what's working and what's not working to identify areas of improvement.

WOM School Story Marketing plans and teams will look different for each school. With that in mind, you need to remain flexible and be open to adjusting your plan so that it fits with your school's goals and culture. You also need to determine how to effectively maintain your efforts.

How to Effectively Execute and Manage Your WOM School Story Marketing Plan

Now that you're armed with what you need to develop your WOM School Story Marketing plan, let's take a look at what it takes to keep it going in the long term.

Executing the practice of WOM School Story Marketing in a school is kind of like planting a vegetable garden. You add some compost to your soil, choose some healthy seedlings, and give them plenty of water. In a couple of months, you could be handing out zucchinis to anyone who wants them. On the other hand, you could be pulling up dead plants and wondering what happened.

It's hard to know exactly what outcomes your WOM marketing efforts will produce down the road. You can consider various strategies, gather a team, plan a kickoff meeting, decide which tools to use. But, the fact remains,

WOM School Story Marketing is not something you can apply a formula to and expect a certain result.

Each school's WOM team will be different. However, at Schola, we've noticed trends and typical scenarios among the teams we've been involved with. Based on that experience, I'd like to share some secrets, tips, and tools we've picked up about WOM marketing along the way. Let's start with some secrets.

Three WOM School Story Marketing Secrets

Secret #1: WOM School Story Marketing is Vague

Not only is it vague, but because it is so relational, the outcome is heavily dependent upon the people involved in telling your story.

The key to success in WOM School Story Marketing is to provide your team opportunities to talk to one another. Give them the chance to share what's working well for each of them and what might not be working quite so well. This sharing will lead to insights that can help all your team become better storytellers. Here are three ways that can happen:

1. **Stronger storytellers can model the process**
    For some, their lack of success might not be a result of the stories they tell, but how they're telling them. Identify those who have mastered the process and have them model that process for the others.

2. **Individuals can collect more stories**
    Team members have the chance to add to their collective storybooks when they share their own stories with one another. This can be especially helpful for team members who are having a hard time relating to some acquaintances. For example,

a parent of a high schooler might find it hard to engage with a friend who has preschool-aged children; however, that same parent, armed with a personal story about a team member with a kindergartener, is more likely to forge a meaningful connection.

3. **Everyone can learn how to tell more impactful stories**

In some cases, individuals may only know parts of a story. In others, they might not see all the connections. Talking through stories together gives the team a chance to fill in the gaps to be able to tell those stories in a way that packs more of a punch. For example, everyone may be familiar with the story about the alumni serving as a pilot in the Air Force, but does everyone know that the seed for that desire was planted during a career day event he took part in when he was a fourth grade student at your school? By taking the time to share these stories, stories of alumni who are successfully living out their callings, teachers faithfully mentoring and discipling their students, and discovering the connections that exist, your team can connect the necessary dots to tell those stories in a much more impactful way.

Secret #2: WOM School Story Marketing is an Antidote to Negativity

Unfortunately, despite your efforts to delight your current families, you're bound to come across some naysayers within your school community. It's difficult to please all the people all the time, and when parents are paying tuition, many times; they don't hold back their opinions.

Take the opportunity to feed your WOM team some good news stories that may arise out of an unpleasant situation. Consider this story:

The original plan at one school to paint the walls and replace the carpet in their kindergarten suite led to the discovery of a mold issue that needed to be addressed. One thing led to another, and the plans for a minor cosmetic upgrade quickly morphed into a major renovation project; a project with a cost projection well beyond what the school, one facing financial challenges to begin with, could afford.

Through what could be described as none other than a series of small miracles, between a little-known grant opportunity and proceeds from a special memorial fund, the school was able to not only resolve the mold issue, but also restructure the classroom space to create a more conducive learning environment to support the new kindergarten curriculum the school had just adopted.

To celebrate this momentous occasion, the school held a special open house and invited community members, both old and new, to join in on the festivities and share in the story. The event created quite a buzz, and the new curriculum and space became a big selling point in their efforts to grow school enrollment.

Secret #3: WOM School Story Marketing is Contagious

WOM team members are tuned into the positive things that are happening around campus and in student's lives. In a subtle way, they are taking the vision and mission of the administration and school board and are humanizing it through their sharing of stories. And when satisfied parents start sharing examples of transformation actively and intentionally, it has the power to change the climate of your school in a positive way.

Prepared to mourn the loss of one of their staunchest WOM advocates upon her youngest child's graduation from their school, those overseeing the school's WOM program were beyond elated to learn that their star storyteller, Ann, had absolutely no intention of quitting the team. The fact that she willingly and eagerly returned to speak at enrollment events in and of itself was a powerful testimony to the impact the school had in the lives of her children and family. And the fact that Ann was still there even though she no longer had children at the school did not go unnoticed by either the current or prospective families who attended these events. Neither did her inspiring and heartfelt stories.

Those are some of our WOM School Story Marketing secrets. Now for some tips.

Three WOM School Story Marketing Tips

Now that the secrets have been revealed, it's time for a few WOM tips.

Tip #1: Examine Your Customer Service

While prospective parents who interact with your school may not be members of your WOM marketing team, they are likely to talk to their friends or family members about their impressions of your school. Based on their experiences, what do you think those prospective parents might be saying about your school?

Over the years, I've conducted a number of "secret shopper" calls and school visits, and let me tell you, there are quite a

STORY MARKETING FOR CHRISTIAN SCHOOLS | 117

few negative things I could say about some of those schools based on my experiences.

For those entrenched in the day-to-day work of your school, it's difficult to relate to an outsider who calls or visits your school for the first time. Considering the daily challenges your staff face in juggling multiple tasks while having to put out the inevitable fires that always seem to pop up at the most inopportune times, it's easy to understand that fuses can wear a bit short. However, if you want to make a good impression on potential enrollment prospects, it's extremely important for any and all who might interact with them to be able to step out of their own shoes and into the prospect's shoes when necessary. And to be understanding, positive, and helpful.

In addition to conducting phone training with those who regularly answer calls, one school we worked with created a phone script that was housed in a prominent location near the front desk for anyone who might be asked to help out with answering the phones when unexpected needs arose. Included at the bottom of that script were the names and extensions of key staff members, who could answer admissions questions. That way, if a question could not be answered by the one who took the call, the call could be transferred to someone who could. This training and tool offered guidance and instilled confidence in staff members for them to be able to quickly and efficiently address the prospect's needs.

Examine the ways in which your school personnel are communicating with your prospective parents. Are they being greeted warmly and respectfully? Are they being made to feel understood and valued?

Are systems in place to ensure each prospect is followed up in a timely manner? Do you haphazardly approach prospects like they're already familiar with your community traditions, buzzwords, and culture? Or do you take the time to understand their needs and motivations and address them based on where they are in their buyer's journey?

For example, rather than starting off the conversation with a family who is attending their first open house with details about your application process, begin by asking them a few questions, including what led them to attend your open house. The answers you receive may indicate they aren't far enough along in their exploration process to even be thinking about filling out an application. By taking the time to listen to them, rather than turning them off by pushing them into something they're not ready for, you are in a better position to address the true needs and concerns they have at this particular point in time.

Tip #2: Give Clear Expectations

Ever ask your child to clean up the kitchen and return only to discover that the stack of dirty dishes you expected to be gone is still piled high in the sink? When you confronted him, you learn he thought you simply meant for him to put the cereal boxes away?

If you want your WOM team to be successful in their efforts, you need to give them clear direction. Don't be shy about it; however, do allow room for their personality and creativity to shine through. It's helpful if they understand the time and deadline parameters, and show them good examples of what you want their end result to be.

One school maintained a binder that contained planning details for previous enrollment events. This proved to be extremely helpful when others took over the event planning duties as it provided a template that could be followed and adapted to meet current needs.

Tip #3: Help People Find Their Lane

Putting together a WOM School Story Marketing team is much like coaching a softball team. You have a bench full of a variety of personalities, interests, and skillsets. As a coach, your job is to figure out the best position for each of your players.

Assist your team members in identifying their relational or speaking abilities and provide training to prepare them to help with prospective parent events at your school.

Depending on their talents and interests, they might enjoy giving a testimonial to school visitors, leading them on a campus tour, or overseeing the refreshment table at your open house events.

If you have team members who may not be comfortable speaking in front of a group, encourage them to write testimonials to post on school review sites or social media channels.

Others with connections in the community may enjoy visiting churches, real estate offices or pediatrician offices and chatting with them about the school. We've had a number of schools create promotional posters and brochures that individuals like these can leave behind at the locations they've visited.

Your WOM team members will be most effective when they're each involved with work they enjoy and can manage. With the tips revealed, it's now time to share some more tools.

Three WOM School Story Marketing Tools

Here are a few more tools to add to your WOM School Story Marketing toolkit.

Tool #1: Rack Cards

How can your WOM team spread the word once you've scheduled prospective family events? One idea is to create a rack card that lists the dates and times for these events and ask your team to distribute them to doctors and real estate offices, churches, and directly into the hands of prospective parents with whom they are talking about school options.

Including several events on the same card can be more cost-effective than creating a card for each individual event. However, you need to plan enough in advance in order to do so.

An inbound marketing-friendly tip is to include a site link on the rack card for an offer, such as a checklist or ebook, which includes information to help parents research school options in your particular town. Whether or not they choose to attend any of your events, this offer may entice them to visit your website and potentially become an enrollment lead.

Tool #2: Parent Ambassadors

Take the time to invest in grooming an enthusiastic cadre of parent ambassadors who can assist you in executing successful open house events and tours. These parent ambassadors can be trained to assess prospects' challenges and provide possible solutions as they lead them on a tour of your campus. By giving prospective parents access to current ones, they have the chance to learn how your school is impacting children in the community from someone who has once walked in their shoes.

Several schools we've worked with have made the extra effort to pair prospective parents with current parent tour guides who have children in the grades they are considering. This gives the prospective parents the chance to pose questions about the teachers, programs, and curriculum to someone with current working knowledge and experience regarding the subjects in question.

Tool #3: Online Reviews

With today's technology and so much information at their fingertips, many prospective parents are more than halfway through their buyer's journey before they even make contact with a school to schedule a visit. And it's highly likely that most of their decisions up to that point have been determined based on the research they've conducted online. With that in mind, it's extremely important to foster your online WOM efforts by having a positive presence on the various online school review websites.

Millennial parents are especially likely to consider the thoughts and opinions of peers before making a purchase.

Do you have a school profile on sites such as great-schools.org? Do these sites include up-to-date testimonials from satisfied parents? If not, assign the completion of this task to your WOM team.

Why do online reviews matter for school word-of-mouth marketing? Let me provide an illustration:

Once, while on a business trip, my son informed me that a mishap had occurred with my lawnmower. I came home to knee-high grass and neighbors' angry stares because of it. After spending the better part of the weekend scouring YouTube and Google for do-it-yourself solutions, I soon realized I was not going to be able to fix the mower on my own before having to leave for my next business trip. As a result, I modified my efforts and began the search for a local repairman who could get the job done quickly.

The most compelling factor in my selection of a repair shop had to be the reviews I read on Google. As a matter of fact, the reviews were so positive for my shop of choice that when I contacted them, I learned they had a repair backlog of three weeks! Knowing my sense of urgency, the shop owner gave me a word-of-mouth reference for another local repair shop. Fortunately, I soon got my mower back in working order and the jungle in my yard was promptly restored to its rightful state, much to my neighbors' relief.

You may have encountered situations similar to my own experience, situations in which you reached your pain threshold, and a solution was very much needed. In a similar sense, when prospective parents' pain points and frustrations have reached the breaking point, their quest for a solution often leads them to go online to seek answers to their educational challenges. When that happens, you want to be sure you're the school they find. And one of the easiest ways to accomplish this is to make sure your current families are writing reviews of your school and posting them on the various school review websites and social media platforms.

Why are reviews so important when it comes to helping your school get found online by prospective parents? Here are four reasons:

1. **Reviews are trusted by prospective parents and empower WOM School Story Marketing**

   Ratings and reviews play a huge role in a prospective parent's decision, one way or the other, about your school. Remember: People talk. Friends and family listen and trust what is being said. So, they take action.

   When current families write reviews, they are providing social proof that you are trustworthy. Don't miss out on a golden opportunity to get ahead of your competitors by recruiting your current parents to do more online reviews. And this is especially important when it comes to attracting millennial parents who rely heavily on feedback through online social networks when making purchase decisions.

2. **Google My Business features reviews prominently**

   Have you ever seen the maps that appear when you conduct a Google search for a local business? They're typically located at the top of the search engine results page (SERP). Wonder why some businesses and schools appear on the map while others do not? According to Google, reviews have a huge impact on the prominence your school gets on the map. So, the more reviews your school gets, the higher the chances you'll appear on the map.

3. Ratings and reviews can influence rankings

Not only are ratings and reviews valuable for the reader; they also indicate to search engines that your school is valued by others in the local community. In addition, when reviews and ratings appear on multiple sites, it increases your online footprint, which is extremely beneficial for your search engine optimization (SEO) efforts and, ultimately, your overall ranking results.

In other words, the more reviews and the better the ratings you get, the better the chances that your school will move up in organic rank. To increase your online visibility, create a list of sites to focus on. Examples include Google reviews and third-party sites, such as greatschools.org and private-school-review.com. And don't forget to include the review section on your school's Facebook page. The more you target, the greater the impact you'll have in increasing your school's online visibility.

4. Reviews are mobile friendly

Review counts and average ratings figure prominently in search engine results on mobile devices. And it's no secret that mobile devices tend to be the go-to technology for internet searches. Numerous reports and statistics show that a majority of searches begin on a mobile device and are often followed up on a desktop computer. Ensuring your reviews are easily seen when prospects search online via their mobile phones will make you more transparent and accessible. This will translate into more visits to your website and, if your website design is inbound marketing-friendly, will result in converting more school website traffic into prospects.

When it comes to online reviews, while all the suggestions discussed are valid and beneficial for your WOM School Story Marketing efforts, there is one factor I cannot begin to stress enough, and that is the trust factor. The fact that people felt strongly enough to take the time to write a positive review is a major endorsement for your school. And one that can instill a greater level of trust since it is coming from a source not owned or operated by your school.

There's no reason your school shouldn't have at least 20 reviews online from current families telling others why they love your school, especially if you reach beyond your WOM marketing team to get those reviews. The start of the school year is a great time to encourage your parents to write these reviews. Why? This is generally one of the most exciting times of the year because school is in the front and center of a family's mind and enthusiasm is high.

When it comes to WOM School Story Marketing, there is no one right way, no special formula, and no guaranteed outcome. However, through trial and error, you can discover the right combination of secrets, tips, and tools that are right for your school to be able to reap a bountiful harvest of enrollment prospects.

Once you've determined what's right for your school, what can you do to sustain your efforts over the long haul?

Instant Energizers For Your WOM School Story Marketing Program

Energy and excitement are often high at the start of any new program. However, after a while, the newness wears off, and processes have a tendency to shift into autopilot. What can be done to sustain the momentum and WOM School Story Marketing effectiveness over the long haul? Here are four thoughts:

1. **Audit School Review Profiles**

    A while back, I went online to search for the menu from a local restaurant I hadn't visited in some time. My initial search results didn't yield the menu; however, it did provide a list of sites that included reviews for the restaurant I was searching for. The reviews I saw were good ones, but they looked to be a bit dated. To make a very long story short, through my continued efforts to locate a current menu, I eventually discovered the restaurant had closed several months earlier. Ever since then, one of the first things I do when reading online product or service reviews is to check the date of the most recent review. If it's more than a year or so old, I seriously question its accuracy and relevancy.

    To ensure the information available about your school online is up-to-date and relevant, it's a good idea to schedule periodic profile audits. Take a few moments on each site to update these profiles with current information and photos. If it's been a while since anyone has posted a review, reach out to members of your WOM team and ask them to encourage other community members who have not done so to post reviews.

2. **Gather Quotes**

Which would you trust more, a third-hand account or words directly from the source? Testimonials from current parents or students about the ways in which they are being impacted by your school can have a much greater impact on prospective parents than those conveyed through someone else. Contact a few enthusiastic parents, current students, or alumni and ask them for quotes about their experience at your school. Use these quotes on your school website or when printing items such as brochures and rack cards that your WOM team hands out.

3. **Shoot Video**

Video is another way to build a collection of testimonials. Shoot quick video segments on your cell phone when a family drops off paperwork or is picking their child up from school or a school event. Plan in advance a few questions to ask that will lead to answers from your subjects that may help address prospects' pain points, desires, or challenges. Uploading these videos to social media can provide sharing opportunities for your WOM School Marketing team.

4. **Release Breaking News**

Whenever you have exciting news to share with your school community, such as the hiring of a new teacher or the procurement of a new piece of technology for your school, take pictures, document the details in writing, and pass them along to your

WOM team, so they can share the news through their own social media networks.

Any of these little things can provide the spark needed to ignite a fire to keep your WOM School Marketing efforts going over the long haul. And sustaining these efforts can help your school in other ways as well.

WOM School Story Marketing and Student Retention

WOM marketing efforts aren't just the responsibility of your WOM marketing team. Every member of your school community has the potential to become a WOM School Story Marketer. Continue to delight them, and it's inevitable that they'll "love your school out loud" as well. And the effort you put into delighting your current community can do wonders for student retention as well.

The best time to kick off your efforts is right at the beginning of the school year when enthusiasm is at its highest. The "Back to School" season, September and October, is a time of the year when you have everyone's attention. Your school community is excited and energized to have begun a new school year and is looking for reasons to become your school's biggest fans. It's important to give parents reasons to feel they're part of something special because they are!

Here are some of the ways in which you can take advantage of this excitement to positively impact the conversations taking place with prospective parents and make strides in retaining the current parents in the process:

1. **Kick Your Efforts to Delight Your Current Families Into High Gear**

Believe it or not, at the beginning of each new school year, parents and students alike are beginning to assess their satisfaction level with your school and deciding if they'll be returning the following year. The following are ways you can positively influence those thoughts:

Host a Back-to-School Picnic. An event that offers food, games, and the chance to connect or reconnect with other families and school workers leads to a good time and great feelings for community members.

Create a Buddy Program. Assign parent and student ambassadors to help transition all those new to your community.

Hold a Back-to-School Night. Make it upbeat and brief. Offer opportunities to learn about your various school programs and activities and allow time for classroom visits.

Host a Parent's Day. Honoring your parents and inviting them to visit and participate in the classroom goes a long way in creating an environment of involvement and partnership within your school community.

Utilize Parent/Teacher Conferences as a school marketing opportunity. Empower your faculty to start talking about the benefits of next year's activities and curriculum when they meet with parents.

2. **Recruit a Content Team**

If your school has adopted an inbound marketing strategy, you've committed to creating content to attract prospective families to your school. As you are engaging with parents at the start of the school year, invite potential volunteer blog writers to an informational meeting. You may just be surprised by how many parents (especially millennial moms) already have experience in the blogging world. They may enjoy supporting the school in this capacity.

You'll also need someone to manage that content, so be on the lookout for that person as well. Some schools have hired a parent to work part-time as the content manager or have bartered these services in exchange for tuition.

And don't forget about your school's social media efforts. If you don't have a designated marketing staff member, you may be able to delegate this position to a trusted parent who has a deep understanding and appreciation of your school's culture and brand.

3. **Empower and Equip Your Teachers**

Make sure your faculty is well-versed in your school's mission, vision, and values. Encourage them to share inspiring stories from their classrooms with their friends and on social media, even if they can't name students, in particular, to share your school's story and spread your school's message with regard to how you're working day-to-day to achieve your mission. As I've shared throughout this book, storytelling is a powerful tool that can create a meaningful connection with your audience of both current and prospective parents. And teachers are a treasure trove of the best success stories your school has to offer.

4. **Take Pictures of Your Students, Faculty, Staff, and Facilities**

     Create an image library during the early fall when student uniforms are looking sharp, everyone is happy, and natural lighting is good. Get a variety of photos, including groups, individuals, classroom, campus grounds, sports fields and gymnasiums, extracurriculars, off-campus activities, as well as teachers and students interacting. These images will become a gold mine resource for your marketing efforts throughout the year, and your current school community will enjoy seeing and sharing those you post online.

5. **Create a WOW Moment**

     Think about a way to build unity within your community while doing something unusual to delight your students, parents, and teachers. In other words, do something that will give them something to talk about.

     One school held a pep rally early in the year that included a performance by the school's cheerleaders and mascot. Another that sponsors a House program held an induction ceremony and House competition. Some schools have held a themed day with focused instruction around a specific period in history, such as Colonial America or ancient Egypt, and allowed their students to dress in period clothing for the event.

Consider coordinating other academic-focused events, such as a STEM day or reading festival. Or something as simple as providing each class with popsicles on a hot afternoon. The list of possibilities is endless. While it doesn't matter what you choose, what does matter is the buzz created by stepping away from the normal routine every once in a while.

CASE STUDY:
SUBURBAN SCHOOL EXPERIENCES MAJOR RETENTION RATE INCREASE

Retention Rate Increase from 85% to 97% in 1 Year! New Student Enrollment growth from 17 to 54 students!

Located in Concord, North Carolina, Covenant Classical Christian Academy often heard they were the best-kept secret in town. While somewhat known in their specific location, a suburb 20 miles northeast of Charlotte on the border of a rural area, the school was virtually unknown in the greater metropolitan region and had no idea how to change that.

According to the Co-Head of School, Stephanie Prince, prior to engaging with Schola, the school's marketing efforts were done "on a wing and a prayer." The school had relied mainly on word-of-mouth marketing through satisfied parents; however, what they lacked was an effective strategy for targeting the types of families that would resonate with their mission. Without a firm marketing plan in place, enrollment fluctuated from year to year, and student retention was not where it needed to be.

Unfortunately, this did not bode well for the long-term health of the school.

Prince states, "When we encountered Schola at an Association of Classical Christian Schools (ACCS) conference, we became intrigued by what we saw and began to see how lacking our strategies were and that we needed specific tools and a specific game plan in order to achieve our goals. And that's what Schola brought to us."

At that conference, leaders of Covenant Classical School made an appointment to meet with Schola. During that meeting, Schola team members took the time to explain to them what inbound marketing is, how it differs from traditional marketing, and how effective it could be when used in conjunction with the Schola School Marketing System. School leaders liked what they heard; however, their greatest concerns revolved around one important question: "If we put the money and the effort into this, will it pay off?

By the conclusion of that meeting, those school leaders decided to take the chance.

And that decision turned out to be the right one.

Efforts began immediately with the design of an inbound-friendly school website along with the implementation of systems to track enrollment leads and move prospects through the admissions process. Next was the development of marketing strategies for increasing student enrollment and retention. And those efforts certainly paid off.

"The first year with Schola, we were at a retention rate of about 85%, which we thought was great, but it really wasn't great," states Jan Dearing, Co-Head

of School. "We began our retention efforts immediately and learned so much through the Schola process that first year. As a result, by the following year, our retention rate had increased to 97%, which was incredible. Never have we had that in our 23-year history."

Prior to engaging with Schola, Covenant Classical Christian averaged 17-24 new students per year. At the start of the first school year following their signing on with Schola, the school had enrolled 47 new students. And by the end of that same school year, Covenant had already enrolled 54 new students for the school year to come.

Co-Head of School Stephanie Prince adds:

"In the past, we'd always been going through the entire summer with anxiety about what enrollment was going to look like at the start of the new school year.

This year, we met our stretch goal by the end of April and were poised to exceed that number. Having the peace of mind that those enrollment needs have been met is a wonderful feeling."

And that's WOM School Story Marketing in practice. We've covered quite a bit of ground in this part of the book. Feeling a bit overwhelmed? Wondering how you can apply these concepts and practices to your circumstances? Fear not. In the next section, I'm going to pull everything together with an illustration of WOM School Story Marketing in action and then give you the chance to apply what you've learned through the completion of an action plan to help you determine your own next steps.

PART V:

School Story Marketing in Action

By this point, I hope you're beginning to truly understand what a powerful role storytelling can play in your school marketing efforts. I'd now like to share one more story with you that illustrates School Story Marketing in action. This is the story of one of Schola's clients, their Admissions Director, Suzanne, and the challenges they faced.

This story shows how Suzanne (the hero) takes on those challenges to help her school solve its problems (the external journey) and touches upon the personal transformation she undergoes as a result of the huge barriers she had to overcome (the internal journey). And through it, you'll see how Schola (the mentor) walked alongside Suzanne to help her succeed.

Suzanne's Story

I met Suzanne at the start of a brand-new school year during the initial on-site client visit with the school where she worked as an administrative staff member. A self-confessed Jill-of-all-trades, Suzanne served in a variety of roles at the school, ranging from Development Coordinator to Substitute Teacher to Cafeteria Monitor, roles she often carried out all in the same day. And she was about to take on an additional role, that of school marketing transition team member.

A longtime member of the school community, Suzanne had served in a variety of parent volunteer roles while her children attended the school before she eventually became a staff member once they had graduated and moved on. Because of her deep connection and commitment to the school and its mission, I knew Suzanne would prove to be a key player in helping to assess and address the challenges her school faced.

The Challenge

Suzanne's school, which had literally been built from the ground up, opened its newly purchased modular building doors to a class of kindergarten students in the early 1980s. Through the ensuing years, grades and building wings were added until the school became large enough to accommodate students from kindergarten through the 8th grade.

During those formative years, the school's enrollment grew until it reached capacity at around 325 students. And their reputation grew as well, the proof being the healthy waitlist of prospective students the school was proud to possess. But that success would not last.

A long season of change that included an economic downturn and related financial challenges as well as the departure of a key school leader and the resulting shift in administration led to a steady decline in enrollment. By the summer leading up to the 2013-14 school year, the student population had dwindled to below 200 students. And unless they could find a solution to help stop the bleeding, school leaders began that school year wondering if it might be their last.

The Solution

The solution presented itself at a conference that summer following the school's plunge to rock bottom. Faced with a grim and uncertain future, school leaders met with us, learned about Schola's School Marketing System, and decided to give it and us a try.

Shortly after that, we convened the marketing transition team Suzanne became a part of and began the Schola School Marketing System implementation process at her school.

Schola School Marketing System Implementation

Marketing system implementation involved three phases: assessment, planning, and execution.

Phase I: Assessment

We began with the collection and analysis of enrollment and other relevant data as well as a review of systems, processes, and past as well as current marketing strategies.

Through this assessment, it became apparent that, historically, the school had done very little to market itself. People simply found out about the school through their friends and family without much effort on the school's part to draw them in. From this revelation came the desire to become more intentional about their WOM marketing efforts. In other words, to come up with an actual plan instead of just continuing to hope that word of mouth was happening. So, we got right to work on formulating that plan. One that involved creating an overall story-driven marketing strategy to help support those WOM efforts. And one supported by inbound marketing.

Phase II: Planning

Once the school's overall marketing vision, strategy, and goals were established, a plan was devised to help facilitate the system and process overhaul required to support the new strategy. This plan included a website upgrade and "inbound- friendly" redesign to support the inbound metho-dology, the development of buyer personas to better identify and address the needs of the school's target audience, the launching of a school blog to attract visitors to the school website and tell the school's story, the creation of premium content to convert those visitors into leads, and the scheduling of open house events to convert those leads into student enrollees.

The plan also took into account the organizational restructuring that would need to occur in order to have the right people in the right place to execute the plan and carry out the new marketing strategy. As part of these restructuring efforts, Suzanne was named Director of Admissions & Marketing. She was also the one who would lead the charge on the school's WOM School Story Marketing efforts.

Phase III: Execution

With an inbound marketing support system in the works, the school was ready to become more intentional with its WOM marketing efforts.

WOM School Story Marketing: A More Intentional Approach

In conjunction with our efforts to collect the data necessary to create buyer personas, we worked with the marketing transition team to conduct a parent survey that also contained questions to get a read on the current environment as well as current parent satisfaction level with the school.

Between the survey results collected and information obtained through the researching of WOM methods and practices, Suzanne, Schola, and the transition team developed a WOM School Story Marketing strategy. Supported by their inbound marketing efforts, the main focus of this strategy centered around attracting prospective families to attend their "new and improved" enrollment events.

Historically, the school generally hosted open houses two to three times a year. The agenda included the typical information sharing and Q&A session followed by a staff member-led school tour. In an effort to create a more prospect-focused event, we advised the team on ways to offer a more user- friendly experience.

To ensure a consistent flow of leads in the enrollment pipeline, the team decided to hold two enrollment events per month, a morning open house and an "experiential" evening activity. The morning open house events provided visitors an informal opportunity to chat one-on-one with a staff member or parent while going on a building tour when school was in full swing during operation hours. The evening events offered visitors a more structured agenda that gave them glimpses into various school activities and programs through the eyes of its students. For example, one month, participants in the instrumental music program played songs for the audience. Another month, selected second graders presented their history projects.

With a need to attract prospective parents to these enrollment events as well as volunteers to assist with them, the time had come for Suzanne to build her WOM team.

Once potential WOM team members were identified and invitations extended, Suzanne held an interest meeting where she shared the plans, goals, and expecta-tions of the school's WOM marketing plans as well as solicited feedback with regard to which duties each team member desired to take on. And once those roles and responsibilities were established, the school's intentional WOM marketing efforts began in earnest.

To keep the momentum and to ensure the program's success, Suzanne met with her group on a quarterly basis to obtain feedback on the various WOM tactics being employed as well as to share and discuss new ideas and stories. In between meetings, Suzanne connected with the team on a regular basis through informative and encouraging emails.

One of the constants through these efforts was Suzanne's commitment to collecting and relaying stories of how the school was impacting its students, families, and alumni. She and the school's blog content manager worked together to create a monthly "community spotlight" blog series, which proved to be one of her most effective tools when it came to collecting stories. Blog posts in this series featured an interview with a student, parent, staff, or alumni member of the school community that focused on the ways in which the school had made a difference in the life of the highlighted individual.

In addition to supporting and encouraging the team and training them in the art of storytelling, with our guidance, Suzanne tracked and measured the results of their efforts on a regular basis to ensure the ongoing success of the school's WOM School Story Marketing plan.

The Outcome

By the end of that first school year after implementing the Schola School marketing System, the bleeding had stopped. And with regard to their WOM School marketing efforts, Suzanne states:

"We noticed a healthy 'buzz' around the school, internally among staff and families as well as externally in the community. Prospects would tell me that they were hearing good things about the school. And the number of newly enrolled students and retained, existing students both improved."

By the end of the second year, Suzanne's school was poised to begin their next school year with more students than the last, a feat they had not achieved in over seven years.

But that is not the end of the story. Through patience and persistence, the school that one day faced the prospect of closing its doors forever continues to serve its community and carry out its mission to this day more than five years later.

Key Takeaways

Our experience with Suzanne's school and others like it has resulted in the discovery of several key takeaways when it comes to effective School Story Marketing.

To be successful in your own School Story Marketing efforts, you need to:

1. Lay a Solid Foundation

To execute an effective marketing plan, you must first clearly define your goals and establish the systems and processes required to support your efforts. You also need to identify and clearly define the expectations of the people involved as well. But most importantly, you must be prepared to make adjustments along the way when necessary.

2. **Become a Change Agent**

While change is inevitable, it is not always easy. Be proactive in managing that change by focusing on the value of the transformation that is taking place. Be prepared to provide the support required to facilitate that change by maintaining a pulse on the environment and taking action where needed.

As an example, when Suzanne moved into her new position as Admissions & Marketing Director, she continued to carry out some of her previous duties, including Cafeteria Monitor. This role proved to have an adverse impact on her ability to carry out her admissions responsibilities when she discovered that many of the calls she placed to prospective parents were being returned during their own lunch hour while she was away from her desk. As a result, changes were subsequently made that freed Suzanne up to be available for those calls.

3. **Be Prepared to Make Some Hard Decisions**

Despite your best efforts to be an effective agent of change, it's highly likely you'll still encounter your fair share of negativity and naysayers. And this negativity may lead you to face some tough decisions.

In addition to Suzanne's move to a new role, the implementation of the new system led to a shift in the responsibilities of several other staff members as well. While some, like Suzanne, embraced these changes, others pushed back. Hard.

Some of those who pushed back lacked the skills required to carry out their new responsibilities. And their desire to cling to "the old way" of doing things made it difficult for others to carry out their new roles effectively. As a result, school leaders were faced with some tough staffing decisions. Unfortunately, there were no simple solutions, especially since some of those naysayers were longtime employees with strong ties to the school.

To address negativity, find ways to shatter the false beliefs of those still set on the "old ways." For example, have those who've embraced the new approach share stories of their "aha" moments and successes with the rest of your staff.

If the negativity persists, be prepared to face some tough decisions. And face them you must, or you just might put the long-term success of your efforts in jeopardy.

4. **Prepare For the Long Haul**

Intentional WOM School Story Marketing takes time, so don't expect immediate results. Think marathon, not sprint. And encourage the rest of your community to do the same. Your efforts will be well worth the investment. Just be patient.

Because of the long-term nature of this type of endeavor, patience will inevitably run thin at times, and it may become quite difficult to stay the course. Make an effort to maintain a positive attitude and celebrate each win. Acknowledge the hard work that is taking place and, above all else, continue to maintain a level of trust by keeping the lines of communication open.

5. **Cultivate a Culture of Storytelling**

As I've stressed throughout this book, storytelling is one of the most compelling and effective ways to connect and build trust with your enrollment prospects.

Educate your school leaders and other influencers on the value and importance of storytelling, so they can help lead the charge. Use the examples shared throughout this book as a starting point for creating your own intentional system of story collection and sharing. Train up storytellers, equip them with the stories you collect, and empower them to come up with their own.

Conclusion

With the insights I've shared throughout this book, my hope is that you are now better equipped to embark upon this journey that will surely pay dividends for your school in terms of satisfied families and a growing school community. I want to encourage you to continue to explore how the practice of School Story Marketing can help you effectively market your school so that you'll no longer be the best-kept secret in town.

As a closing thought, I want to return to where we started. These Christian schools you have poured into to build a legacy of faithful Christian disciples are rooted in your faithfulness to our Lord and Savior and, really, His faithfulness to us, His followers. It is an honor and privilege to serve and build Christian schools all over the world.

However, despite all the creative and cutting-edge techniques offered in this book, they mean nothing if your school is not faithfully helping parents disciple the next generation of young Christian fathers, mothers, husbands, wives, pastors, teachers, entrepreneurs, and workers in any calling. We must always remember that unless the LORD builds the house, it is built in vain. Therefore, we must humbly turn to Him for help in growing faithful Christian schools. I plead with you to remember how your school was established in faith and, whether you have a student population of 2000 or 20, to continue in faith. Our God is faithful to those who will humble themselves and turn to

Him for guidance and direction. May the Lord bless your efforts in applying what you have learned in this school marketing book so that you may continue to be a blessing in your community.

While this might be the end of the book, this is only the beginning. We are committed to walking alongside you on your journey and want you to become a part of our story. I'd like to extend a personal invitation to you to become a part of our community. Please check out the Resource section for more information on how to do so.

Now, are you ready to become more intentional about your WOM School marketing and School Story Marketing efforts? If so, then turn to the next page to create your customized WOM School Story Marketing Action Plan.

Your WOM School Story Marketing Action Plan

The purpose of this action plan is to serve as a starting point to help you become more intentional about your WOM school marketing efforts.

Step 1: Assess Your Current Environment

How do you plan to go about assessing your current environment? (Check all that apply):

~ Parent Interviews

~ Focus Groups

~ Parent Survey

Identify 3-5 questions you plan to ask:

Step 2: Develop Your WOM Strategy

Review your overall school marketing goals and identify 1-2 SMART goals you hope to accomplish through your WOM School Story Marketing efforts:

List 2-3 current or proposed programs/activities that can help you achieve those goals:

What is your plan for educating your school leaders and other influencers on the value and importance of storytelling, so they can help lead the charge?

List the top three false beliefs your enrollment prospects hold:

Identify the stories you plan to share that can shatter those false beliefs:

How do you plan to train your leaders on the process of developing and sharing their own origin stories?

Step 3: Build Your WOM Marketing Team

List 5-10 individuals in your school community who would make good WOM marketing team members (place an asterisk [*] by the 1 or 2 who could serve as team chairperson):

Step 4: Provide the Necessary WOM Marketing Tools

Write your own origin story. Use the following questions to guide you:

- What challenge or opportunity led you to the school?
- Why do you love your school?
- How has being at your school impacted you and your family?
- Why are you so committed to the school?

  If you have/had children attend your school:

- What was the challenge you faced that led you to consider your school?
- What was your "aha" moment that led you to decide your school was the right choice?
- What was the outcome of that decision?

Schedule a lunch date with your admissions team where you will all have the opportunity to share your origin stories with one another.

Identify the ways in which you plan to cultivate a culture of storytelling:

List at least one way you plan to systematically begin collecting stories for use in your School Story Marketing efforts:

List the top 3-5 additional WOM tools you plan to provide your team:

Step 5: Evaluate Your WOM Marketing Efforts

What are the 2-3 main messages you want to communicate from/about your school to the greater community this year?

How do you plan to measure the success of your WOM school marketing efforts?

Notes

Part II
1. https://www.huffpost.com/entry/radio-shack-ad_b_4612973

Part III
1. Pew Research Center https://www.journalism.org/2013/03/17/friends-and-family-important-drivers-of-news/1-word-of-mouth-is-the-most-common-way-people-get-news-
   from-friends-and-family/
2. Nielsen https://www.nielsen.com/us/en/insights/news/2015/digital-formats-are-among-the-most-trusted-advertising-sources-despite-slow-growth.html
3. Nielsen https://www.nielsen.com/us/en/insights/news/2013/under-the-influence-consumer-trust-in-advertising.html
4. Sernovitz, A. (2006) **Word-of-mouth marketing: How Smart People Get People Talking**. USA. Kaplan Business.

Part III
1. https://thechickenwire.chick-fil-a.com/inside-chick-fil-a/the-big-stories-behind-the-little-things

Part IV
1. Harvard Business Review https://hbr.org/2003/12/the-one-number-you-need-to-grow
2. Sernovitz, A. (2006) **Word-of-mouth marketing: How Smart People Get People Talking**. USA. Kaplan Business.

Resources

It's nice to read a book and get creative ideas. However, creative ideas don't generate results, but effectively implementing those ideas will.

The team at Schola Inbound Marketing is focused on getting results for schools. I want this book to be a starting point in helping you take the next step. As a result, I have asked my team to recommend the top resources Schola uses to help our premium and mastermind Schola University clients.

Below is a link to a special page on our website just for those who have taken the time to read the book and want to take action. Implementing the items you find on this page could easily help you increase your enrollment rate by 5 to 10 students and generate over $100,000 in tuition revenue.*

This assumes an average tuition is $10,000 year x 10 students I encourage you to take the time to look at these resources as it could make a big difference for your school. To access this page and these valuable resources, please go to https://www.schoolstorymarketing.com/resources to create an account and log in.

Made in the
USA
Middletown, DE